CONTENTS

Preface	5
Introduction	6
Liverpool Museum and the Pilkington's com...	7
The museum's intent	9
How the tiles were made and fixed - a veritable chef d'oeuvre	11
Choices, costs and delays	13
The museum view - the costs	17
Pilkington's view and the council's decision	17
The installed panels - pottery through the ages	19
The Babylonian panel - the Palace of Sargon	21
The Chinese panel - and the Silk Road	27
The Persian panel - "exceptionally beautiful"	35
The Greek panel - patterns for the civilised world	47
The Roman panel - pottery of conquest	55
The panels that never happened	60
The Italian panel - forms so wondrous fair	60
Panels 2 and 9 - the Egyptian and the early English	65
The Liverpool panels - connections with the potter's craft	66
The Prehistoric panel - "clay created the potter"	69
The Liverpool blitz and the Goddess of Destruction	73
Pilkington's, a Lancastrian pottery	78
How this work came about	82
Notes	83
Acknowledgements	89
Photographic acknowledgements	90
Select bibliography	90
Plans of the museum	92

PREFACE

After my inspection of the boarded up Forsyth panels at the badly war damaged Liverpool Museum in the 1950's and the subsequent decision by both Pilkington's and the Museum that it was not financially practical to try to salvage the panels, I thought that that was the sad end of a glorious story.

However, thanks to the generosity of Pilkington's Tiles Limited and to the persistence of several individuals, not only have wonderful full size original cartoons for six panels been found at the factory but these have now been photographed, using digital enhancement in some cases, and the actual cartoons have been given by Pilkington's to Salford Museum and Art Gallery. It hopes to restore these to their original state and eventually to put them on display

Thanks to the diligence and scholarship of Angela and Barry Corbett the whole fascinating story of the Forsyth Tile Panels for Liverpool has been recorded in this book. Their account sets the scheme in its historical perspective and illustrates the huge commitment of time and detailed research that the Company was prepared to put into such a major project.

Gordon Forsyth was an outstanding ceramic artist and teacher and under the direction of William Burton he ran the Design Studio at Pilkington's during its golden age. The period from the late 1800's through to the first war was a wonderful flowering of artistic style and creativity and Pilkington's reflected this with a magnificent outpouring of exciting pottery and tiles making the Company world famous. The Liverpool project came at the end of this time when Forsyth was at the height of his powers and was undoubtedly his greatest work in tiles.

The authors are to be congratulated for this wonderful work and for the commitment and dedication that they have put into it. I am proud that I was able to play a small part in the redemption of the cartoons and that the Pilkington's Lancastrian Pottery Society has supported the authors and published this historic book.

Lawrence Burton MBE

January 2004

At a Meeting
of the Council of the City of Liverpool, held on Wednesday the 7th day of May 1913

INTRODUCTION

"At a Meeting of the Council of the City of Liverpool, held on Wednesday the 7th day of May 1913 ..." it was decided to commission extensive alterations to the City's Museum and surrounding buildings.

This book tells the story behind the installation of five tile panels depicting the history of pottery which were "entirely out of the ordinary in tile production." A further four panels which were part of the same scheme were proposed but not installed. Complete artwork for two of these exists. A related scheme for two panels celebrating Liverpool's once significant connection with pottery did not proceed beyond the original sketches.

All were commissioned from Pilkington's Tile and Pottery Company Ltd. (currently Pilkington's Tiles Ltd.) at Clifton Junction, Swinton, near Manchester, Lancashire.

This is also the story of the panels that were not installed: why they were proposed and why were they not commissioned.

When these works were proposed, the City of Liverpool and Pilkington's were both at their peak. Pilkington's, managed by the charismatic William Burton, had been awarded a Royal Warrant in 1913.

William Burton was a young man in 1891 when he was asked to take the position of managing director at Pilkington's - a new pottery outside the traditional confines of Stoke-on-Trent. By 1913 his star had been rising steadily. He was a noted authority on ceramics. He was a pioneer of the use of leadless glazes[1] and tireless in his pursuit of improvements in the working conditions of pottery workers. He had lectured in major cities and often featured within the pages of *The Pottery Gazette*. He had also been involved in establishing the Tile Manufacturers' Association.

Pilkington's artists were directed by Gordon Mitchell Forsyth, an acknowledged teacher, designer and leader in his field.

Liverpool's first museum, in Duke Street, was founded in 1851 "dedicated to inspiring people with new knowledge."[2] It had a worldwide reputation. When a new museum, in William Brown Street, was established its objective was to "stimulate and broaden the mind."[3] In 1913 Liverpool was a thriving port and an important city. The tile panels were a testament to the ambitions of this museum and the people of Liverpool. This book seeks to capture the background to that ambition.

In 1941 Liverpool suffered one of the worst nights of bombing in the Second World War which destroyed much of the fabric of the museum. As a consequence the panels themselves could not be saved and only a small fragment of one panel and some original art work survives.

The modern Liverpool Museum reopens in a newly adapted and improved building in the near future. New plans for the original artwork bring our story up to date. It is appropriate to record this part of the museum's history.

LIVERPOOL MUSEUM AND THE PILKINGTON'S CONNECTION

The Duke Street building served both as a museum and library for eight years and it soon became evident that the building was not large enough. The initial zoological collection, presented by the 13th Earl of Derby, attracted 5,000 visitors a week and by 1855 it was recorded that:

> "Advantages afforded by the collection are not confined to Liverpool but are also enjoyed by many thousands of persons resident over a large portion of the country."[4]

In 1853 a new site was found on the north side of Shaw's Brow (which had been the site of a pottery many years before). The building was funded by a gift from William Brown, later Sir William Brown, who had made his fortune in the family business of the linen trade. He was elected to a council post and later served as a Member of Parliament for South Lancashire until 1859. Brown's gift to the city was reputed to have been £40,000 and was to cover the costs of the museum and the public library.

Sir William Brown

Thomas Allom was the architect for the new museum which opened on 18th October 1860. The day was marked by a public holiday. It is recorded that Mr. Brown had suggested that "a portion of the new building might be advantageously appropriated for the exhibition of new patents and improvements of a scientific character."[5]

The museum's success grew. Within two years it was attracting almost half a million people a year. By 1906 it attracted international acclaim as "next to London, the most comprehensive and in all respects one of the best in Great Britain."[6]

Its chairman stated:

> "It should preserve for future study material on which studies have been made in the past, in order that those results may be confirmed, corrected or modified."[7]

On the 7th of May 1913, the city council declared its support for a significant improvement scheme. The proposal involved borrowing £9,000 and was:

> "...for the purpose of improving the entrances, alterations, &c, and better means of communication in the Library, Museum and Art Gallery buildings, in accordance with the plans proposed by Messrs. Briggs, Wolstenholme and Thornley...."[8]

By this time a technical college had also been established on the ground floor of the museum building.

In the same set of council minutes, (along with approval for a curator to spend six months in Kuala Lumpur and for the provision of "loose calico covers") was approval for the curator to attend a Royal Academy exhibition "and visit other Exhibitions etc., in London and elsewhere."

Pilkington's had already undertaken a significant commission in Liverpool in 1903.[9] The Lister Drive Baths in West Derby, Liverpool, were opened to considerable acclaim. Pilkington's was responsible for the tile work, some of which was by the celebrated architect and designer C.F.A. Voysey.

An exhibition of pottery in 1904 at the Henry Graves Gallery in London was widely and favourably reported in *The Studio* magazine[10]. In 1908 Pilkington's lustreware and its stand at the Franco-British Exhibition (designed by the noted architects Edgar Wood and J. Henry Sellers) had been a triumph. They had exhibited twice at Liverpool. Reviewing the Crafts Exhibition at the Old Bluecoat School, Liverpool, *The Studio* noted especially the "many designs by Walter Crane[11], Forsyth and others."[12] The same journal reviewed the Walker Art Gallery Autumn Exhibition in 1912 and paid tribute to Gordon Forsyth and his "high standard of accomplishment."[13] (Forsyth was highly regarded and had been illustrating the soft back covers of *The Studio* for some years.)

The Liverpool Daily Post and Mercury records this review of "The Liverpool Exhibition – Palace of Applied Arts opened 3rd June 1913":

> "apart from the Stoke-on-Trent exhibits, the pottery section includes various delicate specimens of lustre ware contributed by Messrs. Pilkington's ... and Ruskin."[14]

Following a visit by the King and Queen to the Earl of Derby at Knowsley near Liverpool in 1913 Pilkington's received the award of a Royal Warrant.

The Manchester Courier records that:

> "several of the Royal rooms were decorated with specimens of Lancastrian pottery, the productions of the Pilkington's Tile and Pottery Company, Clifton Junction."[15]

After the Royal Warrant was awarded in September the company took out a full-page advertisement in *The Pottery Gazette* in celebration. By 1913 Pilkington's reputation was well established. In addition to a string of international exhibitions: Winnipeg, Paris, Liège, Milan, Venice, Brussels, Turin and Ghent, there had been notable British exhibitions.

The architects Briggs, Wolstenholme and Thornley were awarded the contract for the museum alterations. The company was well known in the architectural world and especially in Liverpool. In 1907 they had designed the Port of Liverpool Building and in 1909 the Palatine Bank Office adjacent to Brown Street in Liverpool (now Grade II listed).[16] However, there is no clue in any of the correspondence as to exactly who recommended Pilkington's for the work. Their record of success was sufficient to rank alongside other significant tile companies such as Maw, Minton and Burmantofts.

1907 postcard depicting the Walker Art Gallery with the Museum in the distance. (See page 92 for detailed layout.)

THE MUSEUM'S INTENT

Neither Pilkington's nor the museum archives contain any material which would explain why the museum wanted to install decorative tile panels.

Several Pilkington's artists (Walter Crane, Lewis F. Day, William Burton and Gordon Forsyth) had published works on the history of pottery. Numerous historical reviews of the potter's craft were available to the Pilkington's artists at Clifton Junction including a rare work on Persian lustre pottery. William S. Mycock began work at Pilkington's "on tiles" but in his later years lectured extensively about pottery. Richard Joyce had been a school teacher before turning to pottery.

People associated with the museum also had an interest in ceramic history. In 1871 one of its major benefactors, Joseph Mayer[17] (1803 – 1886), published *History of the Art of Pottery in Liverpool* which deals with pottery through the ages from "the antiquity of the potter's craft", through Assyrian, Egyptian, Chinese, Etruscan, Greek, Roman, Medieval, Italian, German to English pottery, Wedgwood and the Liverpool connections. The dedication in the publication is to "James Allanson Picton - Chairman of the Library, Museums and Arts Committee of the town council of Liverpool." (Picton is honoured by the naming of "the Picton Reading Room" within the library.)

Mayer was an important collector. His gifts to the city included a collection of Assyrian and Babylonian antiquities as well as Wedgwood, Liverpool Herculaneum pottery, medieval enamels, Burmese manuscripts, a small collection of Graeco-Roman sculpture and Napoleonic memorabilia. Mayer's gift[18] also included the Egyptian gallery which visitors could have walked through to reach the panels. The panels were to be located on the staircase leading from the Egyptian gallery to the ceramic gallery. Ascending the stairs would, as the museum stated, take the visitor through "a graphic history of pottery."[19]

The founders of the museum considered that a study of the past was essential to an understanding of the future, a view shared by others including Walter Crane who wrote in 1914, presumably at a time when the panels were actually being made:

> "…true originality to be successful can only be achieved by a careful study of the past."[20]

Another important work on pottery, published in 1904, dealt with this historical approach. At that time there had been a significant growth in the number of British pottery and tile makers. W.J. Furnival's book *Leadless Decorative Tiles, Faience, and Mosaic* quoted William Burton extensively and was a significant voice in the growing debate concerning the use of lead in the pottery industry. (The list of reviewers of the work reads like a "who's who" of the pottery trade and they were ecstatic in their praise. Furnival's own "history of pottery" was presented in the opening chapters of the work.) Art, academia and industry were all aligned in a historical approach.

There is however, only one reference to this from the museum:

> "Steady progress may be recorded in the Mayer Museum, and important additions have been made in the various sections. It is proposed to make use of the walls bordering the Main Stairway, leading up from the Large Hall to the Ceramic Gallery, for the purpose of illustrating the history of Ceramic Art, by the exhibition of a series of Tile Panels. These Tile Panels have been designed to illustrate some of the essential characteristics of ceramic design, ornamentation and colouring of the periods ranging from Primitive Man through Egyptian, Babylonian, Greek, Roman, Chinese, Persian and Italian, to Early English times. Two of these panels, the Babylonian and Persian, are now fixed, and three more, the

Greek, Roman, and Chinese, are in preparation and will be completed shortly. Leading authorities in the country have been consulted, and great care has been exercised to make each of them truly representative of the period, not only in the motive of the panel proper, but also in the colouring and in the character of the decorative border. It is confidently expected that, when completed, this series of panels will form an unique exhibition as a graphic history of the development of Ceramic Art."[21]

The museum specifically states that the work will deal with the illustration of "ornament." New printing techniques and new discoveries had produced many works on "ornament" both in Britain and abroad. In particular, works by Owen Jones, *The Grammar of Ornament* and *Examples of Chinese Ornament...*, were essential study for the educated man of the time. New journals, *The Studio* and *The Art Workers Quarterly*, as well as works by Crane and Lewis F. Day were required reading. Works by Binet (Paris), *The Plant in Creative and Industrial Art*, and by Floquet, *Compositions Decoratives,* are all to be found in the Joyce papers at Manchester Art Gallery. The ephemera in the W.S. Mycock Archive at Salford Museum and Art Gallery features other contemporary design sources, e.g., *The Connoisseur* and *Art Journal*.

The museum authorities made their intent very clear. The panels were to educate; they were a celebration of pottery; they were entirely appropriate in design and in location to take the visitor to higher things and greater understanding.

This postcard shows Mayer's Egyptian Gallery. The tile panels replaced the art works at the top of the stairs.

HOW THE TILES WERE MADE AND FIXED
"A VERITABLE CHEF D'OEUVRE"

Liverpool Museum has in its archive a series of letters exchanged between the museum and Pilkington's. It also has six scale drawings of the tile panels (about 22 by 12 inches). Some letters may be missing but what remains reveal a great deal about how the work was commissioned, the estimated costs and the protracted delays. The letters show Pilkington's increasing anxiety about the delays and the threat this posed to the "unity of spirit" of the work.

Pilkington's will have first produced simple illustrated outlines for the scheme. Writing to William Burton on the 27th January 1914, the Museum Director Dr. Clubb states that the museum has all the "drawings" for the scheme bar one. However, in later letters the museum asks for "scale drawings" and Pilkington's request the return of "the original sketches."

In 2003 Lancaster University received further papers from the estate of Mary Chambers, the daughter of the chief designer at Pilkington's John Chambers. Included in these was a set of single and multiple colour prints for the Persian panel and single sepia coloured proofs for the Chinese, Greek and Roman panels. Collectively we have called these the Lancaster prints.

Each is complete and initialled by Forsyth but not dated. It seems likely they were taken from the original uncorrected cartoons. The designs vary from the scale drawings and the final cartoons in their detail. Neither Pilkington's nor the museum authorities mention Chambers' role in the design of the tile panels, however he might have been involved in the project.

No contemporary technical description of the panels is known. Abraham Lomax was a chemist at Pilkington's from 1896 to 1911. In his book, regarding tile commissions, he considers:

"Undoubtedly the finest example of this type of work is the group of five large panels which lined the staircase walls leading to the Ceramic Gallery in Liverpool Museum. Each of the panels represents the contribution of a nation of antiquity to the development of the potter's art, and thus illustrates the great styles of historic pottery: Babylonian, Greek, Roman, Chinese and Persian. All were designed and painted by Forsyth. They therefore show his conception of historic pottery and his ability to translate ideas into material form. They show, too, his craftsmanship, for the tiles are coated with alkaline glaze,[22] which is a very difficult medium for artists because of the brilliance and purity of the colours.

Each panel is 18 feet high and 9 feet wide. Tiles 8 inches square are used for the scenic portion, with narrower tiles for the borders. All of them are plastic-made and slip-faced, painted in underglaze colours, and coated with alkaline glaze. The one representing the contribution of Persian potters is thus executed in their own technique. It is a veritable chef d'oeuvre."[23]

Of alkaline glazes Forsyth wrote:

"Alkaline glazes were much used by the Persian and Syrian potters, and the richness and beauty of their products are well known. It is possible to produce the fine copper turquoise blue only in high alkaline leadless glazes, free from boric acid."[24]

Pilkington's was already noted for its fine Persian tiles. John Chambers designed tiles for the Titanic which Pilkington's executed in the Persian style. Forsyth would have been aware that alkaline glazes were also used on early 18th century Liverpool tiles. This choice of an alkaline glaze was relevant to both the panels and the city.

The process for copying the design onto the tiles involved considerable work in itself. After the cartoons were painted they were "squared up" and the design was traced onto a pounce sheet which is a small sheet of special tracing paper. The paper is pierced along the tracing and the design is then dusted onto a glazed tile surface. The outline could then be painted onto the tile. This technique was common at Pilkington's and many pounce sheets are part of the W.S. Mycock Archive at Salford Museum and Art Gallery.

The W.S.Mycock Archive contains his diaries for the years covering the work on the cartoons. The diary entries are very brief. There are only a few references to the cartoons. On Wednesday 28th January 1914 Mycock notes "Liverpool Museum job came in - two panels for trial." On Friday 13th February 1914 he records "Played golf with Mr.B. in the afternoon. Forsyth had gone to Liverpool." On Thursday 14th May 1914 he states "went to L.Pool to take drawings to the Museum." The final entry is on Saturday 5th December 1914 when Mycock makes a lengthy entry by the standard of the diary: "Worked this and last weekend which together with 2 weekends on the Cartoons makes 6 days."

These entries confirm various dates highlighted in the correspondence though they do not assist us in knowing who else worked on the cartoons.

Probably several different artists, supervised by Forsyth, would have worked on the main image and tile paintresses would have completed the border infills. Pilkington's catalogues for exhibitions in Paris and Glasgow give an indication of the likely approach. After painting, the tiles would be re-glazed and re-fired in the kiln and it is only then that the true colours would emerge. It is possible that at least two copies of each tile were made; Pilkington's made duplicates of important lustre vases in case something went wrong. Whilst Pilkington's had perfected their lustre technique by 1914, the kiln, fired by coal, was still an unpredictable place. The fireman, who was an important part of the team, had only to make a slight error in temperature control for problems to emerge. Similarly, the placing of the tiles could affect the outcome and the kilnsman had a very important role in ensuring that items were placed correctly. The finished tiles would be laid out on the floor to check the alignment of pattern, etc. and then probably numbered on the reverse, packed and sent by train to Liverpool.

The fixing of the tiles was another important job. The company had a team whose job it was to fix large scale commissions. Tiled fireplaces were built at the factory in a slab construction but a different method was used for something as large as these panels.

Lawrence Burton (Sales and Marketing Director at Pilkington's, 1951-1982) explains the process as follows:

> "The first thing to note is that the tiles would have been plastic made i.e. made from plastic clay that was pressed into a tile mould. Plastic made tiles are highly frost resistant, and when fixed by sand and cement, bond so strongly to the cement that in effect they become one. The wall would have had a sand and cement screed spread on it and then the tiles would have been fixed individually using the method known as 'buttering'. This involved spreading a sand and cement layer by trowel on the back of the tile and then pressing the tile home onto the backing screed. The mix would be about 3:1. Sometimes the strength of the mix would be as strong as 2:1 and the result would be that the tile panels would have been impossible to move from the wall using the then known techniques."

CHOICES, COSTS AND DELAYS

The earliest correspondence between Pilkington's and Liverpool Museum has not been found. These documents must have been concerned with the commission and the allocation of responsibility for the work to Forsyth. The first letter in the Liverpool archive is dated 16th March 1913:

> Dear Sir,
>
> I am proceeding with the drawings for the decoration of the staircase, and hope to have them finished by Thursday night. Will you kindly let me know if it will be convenient for me to bring them over on Friday morning, as I understand your Committee meeting will be held that afternoon.
>
> Yours faithfully,
>
> Gordon M Forsyth

The next letter is dated 16th April 1913. In this Forsyth states:

> "I should like to know your ideas regarding the selection of the various subjects etc."

Ideas were exchanged and Forsyth sent a hand-written letter on 20th May 1913:

> Dear Sir;
>
> I mentioned the matter of the decoration of the Egyptian Room to Mr. Burton and he is quite agreeable to my taking up the work if you find it possible & are satisfied with the sketches.
>
> I should be very pleased to submit a scheme of decoration to you & price for carrying out the work if you will kindly let me have the exact measurements & drawings of the spaces. I will endeavour to give you a scheme of a noble and permanent character – worthy of the importance of the Museum.
>
> Yours faithfully,
>
> Gordon M Forsyth

The Egyptian Room was on the ground floor; above it was the ceramic gallery.

There is no further correspondence until 27th January 1914 and then to Pilkington's from the Deputy Curator Mr. Entwistle:

> I write on behalf of Dr. Clubb to say that the scheme for the decoration of the walls over the staircase of the Museum with a series of Tile Panels depicting the development of the Potter's Art as drawn up by you and Mr. Forsyth has every possibility of now being carried into effect.

It would appear that even after a year the authorities had not decided what they wanted to commission.

Mr. Entwistle continues: [Dr. Clubb] "has obtained a sum of money equivalent to the costs of two panels – based on the approximate price given by Mr. Forsyth of £200 a panel fixed and complete." He then requests on behalf of Dr. Clubb that "finished drawings of these two panels [are] prepared and delivered a few days before the time of his committee which meets on Feb.13."

He lists the nine panels that the authorities now wish to pursue and panels showing Liverpool's pottery connections were not included.

They are:

1 The Prehistoric Period
2 The Egyptian Period
3 The Babylonian Period
4 The Greek Period
5 The Roman Period
6 The Chinese Period
7 The Persian Period
8 The Italian Period
9 The Early English Period

PILKINGTON'S TILE & POTTERY COMPANY LIMITED
CLIFTON JUNCTION
NEAR MANCHESTER

WILLIAM BURTON · M.A. F.C.S.
DIRECTOR AND MANAGER

16th. March. 1913

Dear Sir,

I am proceeding with the drawings for the decoration of the staircase, and hope to have them finished by Thursday night. Will you kindly let me know if it will be convenient for me to bring them over on Friday morning, as I understand your Committee meeting will be held that afternoon.

Yours faithfully,

Gordon M. Forsyth

Dear Sir,

I mentioned the matter of the decoration of the Egyptian Room to Mr. Burton and he is quite agreeable to my taking up the work, if you find it possible & are satisfied with the sketches.

I should be very pleased to submit a scheme of decoration to you & prices for carrying out the works if you will kindly let me have the exact measurements & drawings of the spaces.

I will endeavour to give you a scheme of a noble & permanent character — worthy of the importance of the Museum.

Yours faithfully,

Gordon M. Forsyth.

Dr. Carrel
Director of the Liverpool Museum.

He states no "sketch" was submitted in respect of number 1, which is intended to represent "the British potter of the Neolithic or Bronze Age", and adds that number 9 "is a group of English potters of the 17th and 18th century (Toft and Wedgwood)". (Mr. Entwistle implies sketches were submitted for the others. If they were, they are no longer to be found.) In his letter he brackets the Babylonian, Greek, Roman, Chinese and Persian entries with the note: "these are the completed panels". These panels were installed and it is these scale drawings which are at Liverpool.

Concerning panels 1, 2, 8 & 9 Mr. Entwistle adds: "to be done at a cost of £160 each." He concludes his letter by asking for a written estimate of the costs of the nine panels and "also the price per panel."

Pilkington's replied on 28th January 1914. William Burton however, confuses the story by stating in his reply:

> "I will instruct Mr. Forsyth to prepare some sketches for Dr. Clubb and at the same time when the sketches are finished will give you a close estimate in writing for the cost of the nine panels and the price per panel as you suggest."

and he adds a P.S.: "Will you kindly let us have the original sketches back by return."

A letter also dated 28th January to Mr. Entwistle asks: "will you be good enough to let us know whether you require full sized cartoons of the panels for the Meeting on February 13th or more complete scale drawings." William Burton concludes his letter:

> "It will be a very great pleasure to us to do the finest panels it is in our power to produce for your Museum and we are grateful for the opportunity of showing what we can do."

In February 1914 Forsyth writes that he will bring "the two further designs of the Neolithic or Bronze Age and the group of seventeenth and eighteenth century potters, for your consideration." These drawings have not been found.

The correspondence about sketches and drawings ends and both parties seem to have settled on a final choice of the Greek, Babylonian, Roman, Chinese and Persian panels.

In February 1914 Pilkington's Secretary, Mr. Wardle, gives a price of £135 for the first two panels "each net fixed complete." However, he adds:

> "Should we find on completion that this price is too low we reserve the right to amend our price for the remainder of the panels, which we hope will be satisfactory to you."

By 27th July 1914 Mr. Wardle writes to say that Joseph Burton and Mr. Howells will "fix" the Persian panel "at any time". However, on 31st July he writes:

> "that in the prices quoted to you for these nothing was included for the necessary scaffolding owing to an oversight on our part we shall have to include in future panels a sum sufficient to cover the cost of erecting the necessary scaffolding."

Lawrence Burton advises us that estimating the costs of fixing tile panels is a notoriously difficult business even today. Pilkington's was clearly anxious to obtain this prestigious commission but was facing a financial loss with the first two panels.

The Museum's 1914 annual report stated that two of the panels were installed, these were the Persian and Babylonian panels. Discussion on further panels must have been ongoing because William Burton writes in September 1914 that having consulted with "my partners, the Messrs. Pilkington. We are quite prepared to go on with the work and receive the money in reasonable instalments; but we think that the whole sum should be paid in three years, say by November or December of

1917."

Presumably the museum had been restricted to an annual budget. Burton and Pilkington's were willing to help with this problem. William Burton continues:

> "We are anxious that all the work should be completed by the same set of artists, in order to maintain unity of spirit throughout."

This is significant because Burton is implying that, if the council doesn't decide soon, there would be a threat to the artistic consistency of the commission.

He states that he accepted the contract for the first two panels "at a figure that was roughly two thirds of what was offered"; however, "the price has proved considerably too low, owing principally to the impossibility of estimating beforehand for artistic work of this character from small scale drawings". His final paragraph is a model of gentility:

> "I propose therefore, to wait on you personally on Friday morning next when I hope your Chairman and Committee will be kind enough to discuss the matter with me in all its bearings, and if we can arrive at a working agreement that shall be reasonable on both sides, I will afterwards embody our undertaking in writing and we will proceed with the work with all speed. Believe me,
>
> Yours faithfully
>
> William Burton."

It is not clear what happened next. Dr. Clubb was in a dilemma. He had agreed funding for the first two panels but now had to persuade his authority that more money had to be spent.

William Burton must have grown impatient whilst waiting for a decision. On 1st December there is an indication of other problems in a letter from Dr. Clubb:

> "Dear Mr. Burton,
>
> Many thanks for your letter and for the very beautiful print of the Persian Panel, which you have so kindly sent me. I enclose a list of the Museums Sub-Committee.
>
> No one estimates more highly than myself Mr. Forsyth's abilities, aided as they have been by your most able criticism. But we have to satisfy a Committee. I think you will agree that the work in hand covers so wide a field that consultation with varied authorities is compelled. I may not have expressed myself very happily in my hurried letter, but it has produced exactly what I clumsily asked for. If Mr. Forsyth had given to the committee the information and references pertaining to each of the three panels, that you have given, especially for the Greek, it would have been a great help. You do not say if Mr. Forsyth will be here on Friday. If not, perhaps he will let me have similar particulars pertaining to the Roman and Chinese panels and I will do what I can."

Other letters to the museum from Gordon Forsyth provide some detail on the allegorical meaning of the panels and these are considered along with each panel. There is also correspondence with various "learned authorities" including Robert Carr Bosanquet, Professor of Classical Archaeology at Liverpool University and a member of the museum sub-committee. It appears that the committee wanted more detail about the cartoon imagery which Forsyth had not provided. In the end, Burton sent additional information to satisfy the committee's requests.

Matters then seem to have proceeded reasonably well. On 30th April Joseph Burton (William had by now retired) writes to Dr. Clubb to say that the Roman panel is complete and ready to be fixed, "the other two panels are to be finished today", and he wishes to discuss "the question of the remaining four panels."

By 30th April the letters reveal that the Persian, Greek, Roman, Babylonian and Chinese panels have all been completed or committed to. The remaining panels from the original nine are the Prehistoric, English, Egyptian and Italian.

In a letter to the museum dated 11th May 1915 Joseph Burton arranges to visit with Gordon Forsyth and perhaps meet the committee. He also states that he is "glad to hear" that Dr. Clubb "proposes" to get the committee to sanction completion of the remaining panels and again he offers to stagger the payments but states: "there are sound reasons why the work should be done as is generally convenient."

Pilkington's had reached a critical point. They had already spent considerable energy on the project and had begun work on two further full size cartoons, the Neolithic and the Italian, that had not yet been commissioned.

The museum view - the costs

The earlier extract from the museum's report indicates that they had intended to install all nine panels. The costs rose from the original proposal of £135 to more than £200 with fixing, scaffolding, etc. If the museum went ahead with all nine panels they would be incurring costs of £1,700 and it is unclear whether that included all the installation costs.

Putting this in perspective is not easy. £1,700 is nearly 20% of the costs of the £9,000 allocated for the entire building work and other alterations. Another way of looking at this is to relate it to the average wage at this time. The UK Public Record Office gives an example of the wages of male postal employees in 1912. The minimum wage then for a 48 hour week was £1/2/- (£1.10). Pilkington's paid their skilled workers – Richard Joyce, for example – a wage of £3/10/- (£3.50) a week, or £180 a year. Each panel might be regarded as costing a year's salary to produce. In modern terms the venture would cost Liverpool Museum around £150,000. It is perhaps no wonder that they felt costs were escalating.

A postcard showing the Egyptian Gallery c.1915. The installed panels can be seen above the stairs at the back of the picture.

Pilkington's view and the council's decision

Pilkington's, as we have seen, had indicated to the museum that there were good reasons to speed ahead with the work; they wished to preserve the "unity of spirit" of the artists. However, there was more to it than that and this is revealed in a very significant letter dated 31st May 1915 and addressed to Dr. Clubb which was found in the records of the museum sub-committee. The entry is prefaced in the minutes as follows:

"Read the following letter from Mr. Joseph Burton Pilkington's Tile & Pottery Co. Ltd."

Dear Dr. Clubb,
I beg to bring before your notice once more the question of the Tile Panels, for the Museum, and in order

17

that you can bring the matter before your Committee in so concise a form as possible I will give you shortly the principal reasons why I am anxious for the work to be completed

In the first place Mr. Forsyth has not only designed the Panels but he has found it advisable to paint the pictorial portions of the panels himself. It is not at all certain that Mr. Forsyth will stay with us for any length of time, as a man of his ability naturally looks for a larger scope than we can give him here, and it would be a serious matter if Mr. Forsyth left us before these panels were completed. I think you know that we ourselves are very much concerned to have the panels as good as possible and, of course, you are concerned in the same way. I feel it very important indeed, therefore, that we should be able to go on and complete the four remaining panels whilst we have Mr. Forsyth at the works.

In the second place, we are at the present time very short of work for our artists owing to the fact that so little money is being spent at the moment on our higher class work. All our artists (four in number) are married men over military age, they are at present on short time and, consequently, short wages, and it would be a help both to them and to us if we could go on with this work.

There is one other important technical point, - both our artists and the fireman who fires our glazed ware are at present absolutely in touch with all the details of the work and it would, therefore, be much better to have the remaining panels done now rather than to have a break of any considerable period.

I think that your Committee will appreciate that these panels are entirely out of the ordinary in tile production, and we have had to make many trials in order to obtain sufficient technical knowledge to attempt the manufacture of such special work. Now that we have knowledge at our fingers ends I am anxious that some of it should be let slip before the panels are completed.

I quite appreciate the attitude that your Committee took up at its last meeting in reference to this work but I think they will see that in this case there are very special considerations. I hope, therefore, that they will allow us to proceed with the work leaving the question of payment over for the time being.

I should be very glad to hear from you as soon as you can give me any definite answer.

Mr. Forsyth is very anxious to have the sizes of the panels so that he can at least set out his cartoons.

Yours very truly,
Joseph Burton

A resolution was then put to the main council from the Library, Museum and Arts Committee. It sought approval "that the completion of the Tile Panels on the Main Staircase of the Museum be proceeded with". However, the resolution of the Library, Museum and Arts Committee was "referred back to the Committee for further consideration."

By 1915 money for what Burton called "higher class" work had to make way for other priorities. The war was already hitting many homes and was clearly not going to be over "by Christmas." Pilkington's had had to make special war time arrangements and their young men had already been enlisted.

Burton's reference to his artists over military age probably meant Forsyth, Joyce, Mycock and perhaps the tile artist Edmund Kent. However, Forsyth, who was in his thirties, did leave in 1916 to join the Royal Flying Corps. Pilkington's had always been concerned with the welfare of its workers and would not have wanted to dismiss older men from a sense of moral responsibility as much as practicality.

After the war Pilkington's was not the same factory. Not all of the men who had left to join the forces returned. Forsyth eventually left to become involved in the war effort and only returned for a short while. The factory lost skilled men. Probably Joseph Burton sensed that a corner was being turned. In an earlier letter he had referred to the fact that his brother William had retired from the company due to illness. Joseph was left on his own and his colleagues were also disappearing.

Burton's comment about the attitude of the committee is placatory; payment may have been one stumbling block but the authorities did not want to spend this money during wartime.

Burton's letter did at least sway the museum sub-committee because they approached the full council. The council asked the committee to reconsider. In the end they would not sanction the expenditure.

Other factors had caused a general change in attitude towards tile work. The surge in tile production at the turn of the century had lost impetus due to the war. Fashions had also begun to change.

> "The heyday of decorative tiles had largely run its course by World War I… the Modernist reaction against excessive decoration meant more production of plain tiles. The Art Deco tiles of the 1920s and '30s reflected the interest in geometric abstract forms and stylized figurative subjects."[25]

It is not known why the council did not sanction more expenditure; no written record has been found and we can only speculate.

The impetus had been lost. The effects of the war, the lack of money, the change in fashion, their own loss of personnel were all conspiring against Pilkington's. The commission may have seemed irrelevant to a changed world.

The final work consisted of the five panels. Ironically, the work that had been stopped in the midst of one World War was to be destroyed completely as a result of another.

The installed panels - pottery through the ages

Pottery through the ages[26] was a theme William Burton had explored on several occasions in the pages of *The Pottery Gazette*, a very important trade paper, which was required reading for all in the pottery trade. It was the main trade paper for Pilkington's and carried their adverts featuring many important glaze discoveries and the Royal Warrant award.

In a *Gazette* article written in 1898[27] Burton states: "it would be idle to speculate on the place of origin of simple pottery, as all the materials and the requirements needed for its production abound everywhere." However, he points out that when more specialised forms of pottery emerged it was possible to refer to centres of origin. Regarding Chinese porcelain he argues that "all European porcelains were produced in conscious and avowed imitation of the Oriental product." In other lectures reported in the *Gazette*, Burton expands on the various clays used by different cultures.[28] In a celebrated lecture "The Palette of the Potter,"[29] Burton discusses glaze effects and the ability of modern potters to reproduce these effects. Similar themes were echoed in the *Gazette* in 1904, which was a year of particular note for Pilkington's. In that year Pilkington's held an exhibition at the galleries of Henry Graves & Co., London. The *Gazette* reporter considered that "Messrs. Pilkington are now in possession of the secret of the Oriental potter…".[30] Pilkington's began to develop lustre pottery from about 1905 and by the time of the

1908 Franco-British Exhibition this pottery had become internationally renowned.

As the panels presented visually the history of the development of pottery, it was important for the imagery to be correct and understandable. The mistakes that were found in the sketches were corrected by the museum authorities.

Modern scholarship has a much broader appreciation of the history of pottery than that represented in these panels; however, the panels should be understood in the academic context of the time.

THE BABYLONIAN PANEL - THE PALACE OF SARGON

The first panel installed in Liverpool Museum was titled "Babylonia and Assyria".

The Museum had very strong links with the local university and a reputation to protect. Burton and Forsyth consulted several contemporary authorities about the accuracy of this panel. The correspondence throws up many differences of opinion.

Joseph Mayer and W.J. Furnival[31] wrote their own appreciations of the Babylonian and Assyrian legacy – no doubt Burton and Forsyth were familiar with both accounts.

The most recognisable pottery wares of Babylonia are glazed brick reliefs. Furnival includes a description of excavations on the traditional site of the Tower of Babel, "once the famous tower of the seven planets," built by Nebuchadnezzar II, King of Babylon, 604 – 562 BC. He goes on to quote from Professor A.H. Sayce, Professor of Assyriology at Oxford from 1891 to 1915. "...the Assyrians had originally migrated from Babylonia, and that they had carried with them the traditions of the art and architecture of their mother country"[32] and "vast platforms of bricks were used upon which the temples and palaces were built."[33] In Babylonia the platforms and towers were a flood defence. In Assyria it seems these bricks were largely ornamental because there was no need for flood defence.

The scale drawing at Liverpool Museum is titled "Babylonian 1290 – 538 BC". A caption in ink states: "Babylonian: Building of the Palace of Sargon – Glazed Bricks." The lower part of the drawing is annotated in pencil script: "Babylonian Assyrian 3000 – 500 BC." Forsyth wished to depict the link between two cultures.

The Sargon Empire covered the area between modern Turkey, Iran, Syria and Iraq. Sargon was a general term, originating from the Hebrew, meaning "the constituted king". The Palace of Sargon in this depiction relates to Sargon II (a king and great builder of palaces) who reigned after 708 BC.

Almost all the border imagery may be found in the works of Owen Jones, Glazier's *A Manual of Historic Ornament* and Furnival. Small yellow flowers abound in the inner border of the Babylonian panel; these are traditional examples of Assyrian ornament known as Patera, which represent the sun. Assyria was a great wine growing area and the imagery of the vine and the grape in the outer border is common in its monuments.

A variation on a traditional Assyrian Hom or Tree of Life, a sacred plant, is also depicted in the outer border. The Hom was frequently used "as a form of enrichment that influenced much of the later Persian and Sicilian textile fabrics."[34] Owen Jones sources these illustrations to "The Monuments of Nineveh", the ancient capital of Assyria, which, Furnival tells us, was described in the Bible as "an exceeding great city." The repeated border on the frieze at the top is a typical lotus and bud imagery.

Much closer to home, the Pilkington's artists would no doubt have been familiar with Walter Crane's *The Bases of Design*. Here Crane illustrates an Assyrian bas-relief pavement slab from the British Museum. He also illustrates natural forms of vine and fig trees from the British Museum.[35] Interestingly, Crane's work is based on a series of Manchester lectures, which Burton may have attended.

The central image depicts the construction of the Palace of Sargon. The lower part of the building is already constructed and the various decorations, no doubt in glazed bricks or bas-relief, have also been completed. Work is continuing on the upper part of the palace where the scaffold planking is visible. Various foremen and overseers are depicted and more important officials are shown in dress appropriate to their status. The main illustration in the cartoon is explained through the imagery of Assyrian ornament. The regal figure being shaded by slaves in the upper part of the picture reflects a tradition of the bas-relief. The crowned human head was held to represent intelligence and by tradition the figure was bearded. Assyrian statues depicted the ruling king, in this case Sargon, who wears a single rosette on a wrist strap, as a symbol of power associated with the sun.[36] Sargon also enjoyed the patronage of Ishtar the goddess of love and war.

The lower part of the picture depicts a figure of a man with the wings and head of an eagle, a symbol of sovereign power. The man holding a bucket is connected in myth to Aqqi the water-drawer. Sargon, according to legend, was the son of a high priestess who was cast into a river and caught by Aqqi in a bucket. Other images from the Palace of Sargon are a winged human-headed bull, which Furnival illustrates. Legend has it that Assyrian kings hunted wild bulls of awe-inspiring size.[37] The bull itself symbolises a storm and was held to have superhuman powers. In the centre of the cartoon charioteers may be seen hunting the bulls. The use of slaves to transport large building blocks across the Tigris is a part of the Sargon II story. Slaves were also used to transport the statues of bulls to various locations at the entrances to palaces.[38] One of Furnival's illustrations shows "The Lion of Babylon" and this character also appears in the panel.

This panel seems to have produced considerable academic debate which may have frustrated Forsyth who was anxious to start the work. Writing to Dr. Clubb (18th February 1914) Forsyth states that he is returning Professor Bosanquet's letter and asks Dr. Clubb to convey Forsyth's "sincere thanks for [Bosanquet's] kind help and criticism" of his work. Indeed he says that, before starting the Babylonian panel, he will come to Liverpool and have a word with Professor Schwan-Haupt, an expert on Assyrian culture. Forsyth writes to request an interview with Professor Schwan-Haupt again on 21st March. On 4th of May 1914 Forsyth mentions in a brief letter to Dr. Clubb that he is enclosing a list of the "subjects and dates for the panels corrected by Mr. Burton."

A hand-written letter to Forsyth dated 19th May 1914 from Professor Sayce, Queen's College, Oxford, concerns the question of ladders or scaffolding that the Assyrians might have used. Sayce states that he is not aware of any illustration of scaffolding in Assyrian or Babylonian representation but scaffolding "was erected of exactly the same kind as that represented in your panel" in the Egyptian dynasty 1500 BC. He explains that the scaffold was used "where a high wall was covered with enamelled bricks." A sentence is underlined: "I do not see what else could have been used." He adds that the use of enamelled bricks seems to have originated "in [unreadable] & Persia" although no representation of daily life has been found; the Persians were "imitated" by the later Assyrians and Babylonians. He also mentions that in Egypt and Babylonia this use of enamelled tiling "does not seem to have been carried above a man's height." Forsyth sent this letter to Dr. Clubb and says in his letter that Dr. Clubb will note what Professor Sayce writes; "he does not see what else could have been used." It was probably Forsyth who underlined the words in Sayce's letter. It would seem that someone, probably Bosanquet, had suggested that Forsyth might have been incorrect in his depiction of the scaffolding represented in the panel.

This concern with the accuracy of the panels might have stemmed from Professor Bosanquet's determination to have things exactly right. Robert Carr Bosanquet[39] was a member of the museum's sub-committee and a classical scholar.[40] Also in the letter Forsyth stated that he had not heard from Mr. King of the British Museum. The next letter was not sent until 19th June 1914 because Forsyth had said he was going to Paris for two weeks – perhaps amongst other things to study the artefacts in the Louvre. Forsyth again writes to Dr. Clubb to say that Mr. King is "travelling in the

The scale drawing for the Babylonian panel. Courtesy National Museums Liverpool.

The Babylonian cartoon. The canvas is badly damaged and the distortion on the scaffolding poles is caused by the warped canvas. To correct the perspective the digital reconstruction has cut the outer border. Detail of the actual border is shown on the left. Courtesy Salford Museum & Art Gallery.

East" and there had been no reply to Forsyth's letter about the scaffold poles. Forsyth asks Dr. Clubb to pass to Mr King, Professor Sayce's letter about the poles.

It is reasonable to conclude that Forsyth was getting somewhat exasperated with the protracted debate. Three days later (22nd June) he wrote again to Dr. Clubb. Forsyth thanked him for the "letter and drawings" and asked for "a rough sketch of a cross-section of one bay" as "the front elevation" had already been supplied. He adds: "Professor Sayce is of course a very great authority on Assyriology but I will let you have Mr. King's letter as soon as I get it." Finally, in a letter dated 17th July 1917, Mr. King[41] replies:

> "The Assyrians undoubtedly used scaffolding and there is nothing wrong with the general idea of the panel. What is wrong is that the designer has copied modern scaffold poles, obtained from the trees of Northern Europe. The Assyrians would have used poplars and possibly a species of smaller pine from the valleys of the Upper Tigris. The poles would consequently have been shorter, and less regular and straight than those in the drawing.
>
> To get rid of the length of the pole I would suggest finishing off the scaffolding at the main planking, letting the poles end irregularly, at different heights, above the planking; the figures at work on the frieze at the top could be set on a short ladder resting on the lower planking. The designer can retain his awnings, if he wants to, by fixing them to upright poles lashed to the lower uprights. These would serve that purpose very well but would scarcely be strong enough to support an upper planking.
>
> By the way, the ladder shown in the picture is a modern builder's ladder. The rungs of an Assyrian builder's ladder would probably have been nailed into the uprights, certainly not let in like the modern machine-made ladder. Care should also be taken not to suggest machine-cut boards for the planking. As the scaffold was temporary, the roping would certainly not have been so regular nor so neatly finished off. All these changes, I think, could be made without affecting the general design of the position of the figures."

It is difficult to know what changes Forsyth made. We have no date for the Liverpool scale drawings although we may assume they are earlier than the cartoons. The final tile panel was probably altered as suggested.

Forsyth writes to Dr. Clubb on 18th July to say that he encloses a copy of Mr. King's letter. He states that he will "follow out" Mr. King's "few suggestions" and that he had already corrected the length of the poles "before receiving his letter." He then asks Dr. Clubb if "we may proceed with the painting of the panel."

The Babylonian panel was installed and was finally, by common consent, agreed to be an "accurate" work.

Damaged lower border of the cartoon.
Courtesy Salford Museum & Art Gallery.

PILKINGTON'S TILE & POTTERY COMPANY LIMITED
TELEGRAPHIC ADDRESS
TILERIES MANCHESTER
TELEPHONES 4838 & 4938
CLIFTON JUNCTION
NEAR MANCHESTER

WILLIAM BURTON M.A. F.C.S.
DIRECTOR AND MANAGER

19th June 1914

Dear Dr Clark

Mr. *[King]* of the British Museum is I believe travelling in the East & I have had no reply to my letter re. Scaffold poles. I shall be glad if you would give me your opinion of Professor Sayce's letter. I have now after had the measured drawings of the bay of the Central Hall.

We are proceeding with the Persian Panel & expect the first instalment of the finished work out on Tuesday first.

With kind regards
Yours faithfully
Gordon M. Forsyth

Both these images are signed by Fred Wallenberg. They are to be found in the Richard Joyce papers at Manchester Art Gallery. Nothing is known about the artist though the paintings appear to have been inspired by work in the Louvre. Courtesy Manchester Art Gallery.

THE CHINESE PANEL - AND THE SILK ROAD

The artwork at Liverpool Museum is entitled "Chinese: The Introduction of Glazed Pottery into China in the Han Dynasty." The Pilkington's cartoon is captioned "Chinese 200 BC – 1800 AD."

W. Burton regarded Chinese ceramics as those which Europeans most sought to imitate. However, he warns that "whoever would inquire into its origin, the date of its first appearance, or the successive steps by which it was perfected, finds himself confronted by a jumble of incomplete, unsatisfactory, and often mutually contradictory ideas," and also that the "first information of any value"[42] is contained in two letters written by a French Jesuit missionary resident in China, Père d'Entrecolles. Burton quotes several learned authorities including Dr. S.W. Bushell, physician at the British Legation to China for 25 years. Burton explains that the earliest period which scholars can attribute "for even the rudest porcelains" is the Han Dynasty (220 BC to 220 AD). Burton recounts the traditional view that the first Chinese porcelains found their way into the West in the year 1171 when Saladin sent a present of forty pieces to the Sultan of Damascus. At this time, he writes, there existed long established caravan traffic through Mongolia to the ports of the Persian Gulf. It is this traffic that developed into the trade in porcelain around the Mediterranean.[43]

A letter in the Liverpool archive from Forsyth to Dr. Clubb elaborates on the meaning of the panel, which echoes the Burton work. He writes (2nd December 1914):

"Chinese

The subject of this panel is the introduction of glazed pottery into China under the Han Dynasty, which was brought by camel route from Persia and the Nearer East, thus showing the connection between the Ancient Art of Egypt and Babylonia on the one hand and China on the other.

Detail from the Chinese cartoon.

The setting is a Chinese landscape culled from the study of Chinese Art by Dr. Bushell, by Fenollosa and much study of Chinese paintings.

Detail from the Chinese cartoon.

The scale drawing for the Chinese panel. Courtesy National Museums Liverpool.

The figures are composed to carry out the central idea with pottery in the foreground and the camel to indicate the manner of their transportation.

The borders are designed on the Chinese Dragons, which have a symbolic meaning in Chinese Art.

Works consulted include:

Epochs of Chinese & Japanese Art, E.F. Fenollosa.
Chinese Pottery of the Han Dynasty, Berthold Laufer.
Oriental Ceramic Art with Illustrations from the Walters Collection, Dr. Bushell.
Painting in the Far East, Laurence Binyon.
Burlington Fine Arts Club, Exhibition of Early Chinese Pottery and Porcelain, 1910, R.L. Hobson.

I intend to come over on Friday morning in case I may be wanted by any Member of the Committee. Mr. Burton is unfortunately engaged on that day otherwise I think he would like to have been present."

This is a clear description of what the panel represents and it also provides much information as to the source of the imagery. The contribution of each of the above authors is considered below.

In 1913 the City of Manchester held an exhibition of "Chinese Applied Art". In the preface to the catalogue the chairman specifically thanked "Mr. William Burton, Mr. Gordon Forsyth, Mr. John Chambers, and other artists on the staff of Messrs. Pilkington's...".[44] Burton wrote the introductory text for that exhibition.

Ernest Fenollosa was sometime Professor of Philosophy at the Imperial University of Tokyo and Commissioner of Fine Arts to the Japanese Government. He is regarded as the founder of the modern study of Chinese and Japanese art. He evaluated the influence of all cultures on the Chinese, in particular the possible influence of Pacific cultures. However, his view is that with the Han Dynasty "an entirely new set of forces make their entrance into Chinese life, and particularly into Chinese art, which ... takes on new forms ... unrelated to the Pacific."[45]

The name China derived from the Tsin (Sin or Chin) dynasty which ended in 220 BC. After the demise of the Tsin, China became known to the Greco-Roman world as the Ser, or Seres, which was far to the north east of the Tsin. The Sin used sea routes for export through the Indian Ocean and Arabia. The Ser camel trains went overland bringing silk to the West.

Fenollosa argues that it was the Han who exploited both these trade routes to the Greco-Roman Empire. He describes how the Han encountered Assyrian and Babylonian art and in particular the pottery of Persia and the Assyrians. There are many images in Fenollosa's work which could be interpreted as inspiration for Forsyth's cartoon.[46]

Detail from the Chinese cartoon.

Detail from an early Pilkington's vase.

Dr. Berthold Laufer spent nearly three years in China between 1901 and 1904. He had been entrusted, by the American Museum of Natural History, with the role of making investigations and collections in China. The work that followed, *Chinese Pottery of the Han Dynasty*, has since become a classic reference work. Many of the illustrations might have been another source for Forsyth.

In the cartoon the vases appear to have been partly glazed. Laufer draws attention several times to items with various greenish glazes. In his earlier work on porcelain Burton had mentioned the famous greyish-green glazes known to Europeans as céledon [currently known as celadon]; the glaze in the cartoon appears too dark to be celadon.

Laurence Binyon[47] was in charge of Oriental prints and drawings at the British Museum. His work *Painting in the Far East* was first published in 1908, the year of Pilkington's celebrated success at the Franco-British Exhibition. The subtitle of Binyon's work is *An Introduction to the History of Pictorial Art in Asia Especially China and Japan;* "much study of Chinese paintings" mentioned in Forsyth's letter might refer to this book.

R.L. Hobson's work[48] features several illustrations that might be reflected in the cartoon. In particular, the image of a camel is reminiscent as are some of the decorations and the dragons.

In his letter Forsyth cites S.W. Bushell's, *Oriental Ceramic Art*. Published in 1897-1899, in ten volumes it contained 116 colour plates and over 400 black and white reproductions.[49] Bushell recounts a Chinese adage, "Knowledge comes from seeing much," and certainly in Forsyth's cartoon there is much to see and understand.

Bushell notes that porcelain which the Chinese call t'zu is considered to have originated from the Han Dynasty. Porcelain itself is regarded as a Chinese discovery. He lists the various other Buddhist symbols found on Chinese porcelain of which the most frequently used are the eight symbols of good fortune or happy omens.

In the Liverpool sketch of the Chinese panel there is no border pattern. The cartoon however has a vivid border pattern. The Lancaster print is so close in representation to the cartoon and the tile panel that we conclude it was made from the finished cartoon.

At the base of the cartoon the two dragons come together with a geometric motif between. Bushell[50] explains the symbols' meaning in a section entitled "The Hundred Antiques (Po Ku)." The expression Po Ku refers to the infinite variety of ancient symbols and emblems which form a common motif in the decoration of porcelain and other art objects. The motif is called Fu, "a 'Symbol' of distinction to which no special significance is attached and which seems to have been of purely ornamental origin. It is used in the sense of 'embroidered' in modern phraseology, and often occurs as a mark of decorative character."[51] The Po Ku symbols, he explains, are arranged in numerical categories and the most common are the "Eight Precious Things" and the "Four Accomplishments of the Scholar" which are found in the ornamental borders of plates and vases. Bushell lists the eight precious things, which include images that Forsyth put together in this border. If we study the background to the Fu emblem we can see that it is what Bushell describes as "an

Proof of the Lancaster Print of the Chinese panel. Courtesy of the Rare Book Archive, Lancaster University.

The Chinese cartoon. Courtesy Salford Museum & Art Gallery.

open lozenge shape with ribbons entwined around it. This is a 'fang-shêng' symbol, which is a sign of victory or success."[52]

Forsyth informed Dr. Clubb: "The borders are designed on the Chinese Dragons which have a symbolic meaning in Chinese Art." In a section concerning the Po Ku, Bushell lists first the sphere which represents "a jewel or pearl (chu), often drawn with effulgent rays issuing from its surface. The dragon is generally depicted in pursuit of such a jewel. It answers to the Buddhist jewel of the law, the special symbol, also, of a universal monarch."[53]

The dragon (Lung) is usually represented with a scaly body, three claws on each foot and "with a bearded, scowling head."[54] The dragon corresponds to the East, to spring, and had powers of transformation. The Buddhist dragon of the law is depicted grasping the jewel of faith in its claw whilst the "celestial" dragons of Chinese art are seen pursuing the jewels which will give them magical efficacy. Usually this symbol has "positive attributes of spirituality and is a link with heaven. Hence the Chinese Emperors took this creature as their personal emblem."[55]

Bushell explains that the four specially endowed or supernatural creatures of the Chinese are the dragon, the phoenix, the tortoise and the unicorn, and that occasionally the tiger is added.

A considerable portion of the Bushell work is devoted to observations on colour which are summarised in a letter Bushell wrote to Furnival:

> "The symbolism of colour is all important in China. The triple-roofed Temple of Heaven in Peking shines out gorgeously with its pur-

Forsyth's initials on the Chinese cartoon.

> ple tiles, surmounted by a huge purple ball; the sacrificial vases of porcelain are all Mazarin blue, and a subdued blue light is given to the interior by hanging Venetians [blinds] over the window, made of rods of blue glass closely strung together. In the Temple of the Earth, on the contrary, everything is yellow, its typical elemental colour. The roofs of the palaces and the open-work panelled railings of their verandahs are yellow, approaching in tint the deep colour of the yolk of an egg; the princes live in an atmosphere of green. Among Buddhist temples, those of the Lama, the State church, are roofed with yellow; the others under imperial protection are usually green. A general view of Peking from the top of the city wall, which is sixty feet high, shows the picturesque effect of brightly enamelled colours when lit up by the setting sun, the massive roofs of the taller buildings projecting above a thick setting of green trees."

This is the only remaining fragment of the panels. Courtesy National Museums Liverpool.

The dragon border may be seen as symbolising the power of the emperor and the spiritual light of heaven. The other images in the border could have stepped straight out of Owen Jones' work on Chinese ornament which reflects the flora of the country. Flowers have a symbolic meaning in

33

China. For example, flowers in bloom represent abundant harvest: the peony wealth and position, the chrysanthemum endurance and the lotus purity and enlightenment. Such representations were often worked into Chinese fabrics. The small red border is similar in colour to a most striking vase in Bushell's work (Plate XXVIII) which is painted in an "iron red" colour, red being symbolic of the sun. In addition to *The Grammar of Ornament* Owen Jones published *Examples of Chinese ornament selected from objects in the South Kensington Museum and other collections*. This work is described as "selected from Objects in the South Kensington Museum and other Collections." Many of the illustrated border patterns are echoed in Forsyth's cartoon.

The main image in the cartoon is that of a landscape with figures. Landscape paintings in Chinese art present a certain harmony. They often feature a combination of mountains and water and perhaps a bridge, symbolising union. Mountains are seen as objects of veneration but may also represent an impending fall. Forsyth has not adopted the stylistic conventions of Chinese art, but he displays many of the symbols in his presentation of this landscape.

The backdrop to the image represents a magnificent cliff under which traders from Persia and China are seated. The cliff is very similar to illustrations in Binyon's work. Forsyth probably had images of the old Silk Road in his mind when he made this sketch. The deliberate placement of the camel reflects Fenollosa's references to the camel routes of the Ser which later became a part of the Silk Road. The Silk Road linked two continents and spanned China, central Asia and northern India as well as the Parthian and Roman empires.

There were some things over which Forsyth seems to have been very particular. For instance, the merchant is holding a green glazed pot and on the ground are pots with a dripped green glaze. This echoes the knowledge of green glazed wares of the Han Dynasty. The vase is similar to an image in Bushell's work, "... an ancient stoneware of brownish-red paste, invested with a thin but lustrous glaze of camellia-leaf green [which is] a relic of the Han dynasty."[56] The yellow robes of the Chinese merchant may have been chosen deliberately to represent the significance of yellow in Chinese culture. Yellow was used in ancestral temples as an imperial colour; it was also the colour of earth. The whole scene is redolent of harmony and union. The birds in the foreground are storks, which are symbols of the gods; they are also a portent of good fortune.

Forsyth has managed to cram a great deal of imagery into this cartoon. It is perhaps no surprise that the museum authorities wanted a detailed explanation!

Burton had a genuine regard for Chinese art and his conclusion to the Manchester catalogue is apt:

> "Above all, perhaps, one is impressed with the Chinese sense of colour and that profound feeling for artistic quality that has already been referred to, while the gracious dignity of their finest works places them in the very highest rank as artists and craftsmen."[57]

THE PERSIAN PANEL - "EXCEPTIONALLY BEAUTIFUL"

At the Franco-British Exhibition in 1908, Pilkington's stand, designed by Edgar Wood and J. Henry Sellers of Manchester, contained "...painted tiles designed by Lewis F. Day and inspired by the beautiful tile decoration of Persia ... colour schemes of rich cobalt blue, sage green, bright turquoise and Rhodian red." (Quoted in *The Franco-British Exhibition: Illustrated Review, 1908*.)

Pilkington's was established to manufacture tiles. Some of their best work was in imitation of Persian tiles and pottery. The chief characteristics of Persian pottery were very briefly summarised as "rich glazes and flowing lines."[58,59]

There is today at Pilkington's a copy of a rare work by Henry Wallis, *The Godman Collection. Persian Ceramic Art. The Thirteenth Century Lustred Wall-Tiles*, which more than any other work captures the incredible beauty of early Persian lustres.

> "They reveal to us glimpses of the actual East, not the East seen through the spectacles or translated into the language of the West. They bring vividly before us that place of the Oriental imagination wherein is expressed its most brilliant and fanciful conceptions."[60]

Burton writes:

> "At a very early time, certainly as early as the Christian era, the Persians had learned the secret of manufacturing a true glaze, and their glaze was of a very simple composition, consisting of a mixture of clean white sand and either soda or wood-ashes or potass [potash]. Glazes of this nature were very brilliant in appearance, very good for developing colours, and in the case of the Persians, they adhered perfectly well to the ware. One of the striking peculiarities of all alkaline glazes was their extraordinary brilliance. ... From about the eleventh to the seventeenth century the Persians were perhaps the best decorative artists the world had ever seen."[61]

Lustre was one of the most distinctive characteristics of Persian ceramics. Pilkington's was defined by its lustreware.

In 1923 *The Pottery Gazette* reprinted a lecture by Gordon Forsyth on the subject "Lustre Pottery: Ancient and Modern."[62] In this Forsyth repeats the common view that lustreware was first used in Egypt, but was perfected by the Persian potters. The *Gazette's* reporter comments on Forsyth's view that William De Morgan and "in more recent times" Pilkington's "carried the lustre process ... to a great pitch of perfection."

Abraham Lomax devotes a chapter of his work to "iridescent lustre pottery"[63] and as works chemist is well qualified to describe the lustre process:

> "Iridescent lustre is produced by painting on the already fired glaze a compound of silver and/or copper diluted with clay or some other inert material and mixed with some oily or other medium to make the mixture fit for the artist's brush and then firing the ware in a kiln specially constructed for the purpose. At a definite stage in the firing process, described by one fireman as a cherry red heat, the atmosphere in the kiln is changed from an oxidising to a reducing one, restricting the supply of air to the furnace. This is continued for a time and then the fire is allowed to die out. When cool the kiln is opened and the pieces removed to have the inert dilugent washed off."[64]

He describes it as the "most sensitive and difficult" of all pottery processes and says that in a 16th century commentary it was recorded that as few as six pieces out of one hundred might be good. In modern times De Morgan and Pilkington's suffered

PILKINGTON'S TILE & POTTERY COMPANY LIMITED
TELEGRAPHIC ADDRESS
TILERIES MANCHESTER
TELEPHONES 4838 & 4858

WILLIAM BURTON · M.A. F.C.S
DIRECTOR AND MANAGER

**CLIFTON JUNCTION
NEAR MANCHESTER**

2nd June 1914

Dear Dr Clubb:

You will be glad to know that the first portion of the Persian Panel has come out & is exceptionally beautiful & if the remainder of the panel comes out as well you will have a wonderful piece of work.

With kind regards

Yours faithfully
Gordon M Forsyth

Scale drawing for the Persian panel. Courtesy National Museums Liverpool.

PILKINGTON'S TILE & POTTERY COMPANY LIMITED
CLIFTON JUNCTION
NEAR MANCHESTER

TELEGRAPHIC ADDRESS
TILERIES MANCHESTER
TELEPHONES 4838 & 4858

WILLIAM BURTON M.A. F.C.S
DIRECTOR AND MANAGER

3rd July, 1914.

Dear Dr. Clubb,

I herewith enclose a drawing for the colour scheme for the Main Hall of the Museum. The scheme is in light gray green and ivory white. The stone-work I have presumed you will want to keep but it will require cleaning when you have the decorations done. The Capitals are shown in solid gold which should be fairly effective when they are all done.

I shall be glad to know if this scheme meets with your approval but a great deal will depend upon getting the gray green a nice shade.

With kind regards,
Yours very truly,

[signature: Gordon M. Forsyth]

Dr. Clubb,
Director of the Liverpool Museums,
Liverpool.   W

P.S. The Persian panel will be completed on Tuesday first with the exception of about ¼ of the border. It is a magnificent piece of colour & I think you will like it.

**Shah-nama: Banquet Scene Shiraz (c. 1444). J.H. Wade Collection.
Courtesy Cleveland Museum of Art.**

"disheartening" and "grievous disappointments." Lomax explains that what the potter tries to do is to produce a film on a vase that will "split ordinary daylight into its constituent colours." He distinguishes between two kinds of colour. One he characterises as produced by "material pigments," for example, fabric dyes. The other "is produced by light". The colours from light might include "the blue of the sky" or "the rainbow after rain."

This effect is akin to light passing through a prism and splitting into its constituent parts and this "assemblage of many colours is called iridescence." There are many skills needed to achieve this art, from the firing of the kiln to the way items are positioned within it. Pilkington's mastery of these processes was the crowning achievement of the Burtons.

A.J. Cross illustrates many splendid examples of successful Pilkington's lustre. He describes the stand at the 1908 Franco-British Exhibition which "featured tile designs by Lewis F. Day inspired by Persian decoration, and a tile panel of his design ...."[65] The display also featured lustre tiles set in a fireplace designed by Edgar Wood.

John Chambers, Chief Designer at Pilkington's, was responsible for the development of their "Persian" style that brought the company fame and the commission for the Titanic.[66] The Chambers' family gift led to the establishing of "The John Chambers Ceramics Room" in the Peter Scott Gallery at Lancaster University.[67] Many splendid examples may be seen including a set of Cross and Star Persian style tiles in lustre which portray the various Pilkington's artists and are undoubtedly based on Wallis's lustre study. In addition, there are examples of the Iznik pottery that Chambers favoured as well as examples of his "Rhodian" ware which is characterised by red globules of glaze sometimes described as "sealing wax red."

The Persian influence in Pilkington's designs can be seen well before their lustre work. In his introduction to Pilkington's catalogue for the Paris Exhibition in 1900, William Burton described the debt the modern world had to the tile artists of what he termed "the Persians, the Arabs and the Moors." The catalogue also featured Lewis F. Day's "Persian" pattern and the "Persian Tree" and "Persian Iris" patterns.

It is surprising that the actual image in the Persian panel does not show any tiles. However, any reader who needs convincing of the beauty of Persian tile work need only look at the Wallis work referred to earlier. More accessible is the chapter entitled "The Tiles of Islam"[68] in Noel Riley's work which shows stunning tiles adorning the Mosque of Sultan Ahmet and other examples of this art.

Persian lustre is known during the period 800 - 1600 AD. Alan Caiger-Smith speculates that its disappearance in the Il-Khanid empire "may have been hastened by the Black Death which entered Persia at almost exactly that time."[69]

On the 29th June 1914 Forsyth wrote to Dr. Clubb:

> "You will be glad to know that the first portion of the Persian Panel has come out and is exceptionally beautiful and if the remainder of the panel comes out as well you will have a wonderful piece of work."

William Burton wrote to Dr. Clubb on 9th July 1914:

> "I am happy to inform you that the Persian Panel is nearly completed and, so far, is flawless. We hope to have it perfectly finished by Tuesday next and we should like you and Mr. Entwistle and any Members of your Committee to come over and see it laid out because, with your permission, I want to invite some people from Manchester and from the Potteries to see it before we fix it on the walls of your staircase."

No detailed description of the panel is to be found. From Dr. Clubb's letters it would seem he might have appreciated one. In his letter of 1st December he makes oblique reference to it when he says: "if Mr Forsyth had given the information and references pertaining to each of the three panels, that you have given ... it would have been a great help."

It is ironic that this "exceptionally beautiful" panel and also its associated cartoon are in the one case destroyed and in the other "missing". The only representation we have left is contained in prints now held by the Stoke and Salford Museums and Lancaster University captioned "Persian 800 – 1600 AD."

The Liverpool scale drawing for the Persian panel has an incomplete border but a full central panel. The Salford print has a complete border and by any judgement is indeed "exceptionally beautiful." The prints from Salford and Lancaster are identical and copies from this plate may have been given to other important institutions as an example of Pilkington's work.

Perhaps because it has been so accessible this image is the one most copied in various reference books on Pilkington's.

A less well known image of this panel but of great relevance here was included in the catalogue of the 1982 Manchester Exhibition of Pilkington's ware. The exhibition was organised by Richard Gray,[70] then director of Manchester City Art Gallery, which has one of the finest museum collections of Pilkington's pottery.

Forsyth's panel contains numerous traditional references. Part of the border motif resembles a portion of the wainscot of the 16th century Mosque of Ibrahim Aga at Cairo. There is also a great similarity to a 15th century Persian miniature painting, "Shah-nama: Banquet Scene Shiraz (c.1444)"[71] (illustrated on page 39).

The significance of Persian lustre and its "gift" to the potter's world is documented many times in the history of pottery; see, for example, Caiger-Smith and Cross.

Like the Chinese panel the first impression is that of colour, in particular a cobalt blue which was a favoured colour of Iznik production. Iznik is the Ottoman name of the Byzantine capital Nicaea.

The other strong colour in the panel is red, though not of the intensity of the Rhodian reds in a Chambers tile. Furnival states that authorities regard this Persian red as being made by artists at Damascus and on the Isle of Rhodes. The border is made up of various images, all of which have resonance in the Persian ornamental scheme.

The entire border forms a unity, which may be summed up by Caiger-Smith:

> "One of the most favoured Fatimid lustre designs was based on plant forms with spiralling stems, tendrils, palmettes and spear-shaped leaves".

Walter Crane[72] described the use of the palmette shape:

> "To the Persian and Hindu designers, with their exquisite and subtle sense of ornament, with their passion for elaborate intricacy, such a form as this is utilised to its utmost capacity, both in counter-balancing and superimposed masses upon flowery fields, and as inclosures for smaller fields of pattern; while the abundant flora of their spring-time blossoms in a new and translated existence in their richly patterned printed and woven textiles, and in the carved ornament of their buildings."[73]

The predominant and instantly recognisable Persian ornament in the border is the winding leaf with a red centre. This "saz-leaf" motif is said to date from about 1550.[74] Yamanlar-Mizuno traces its origins back to China and a style of drawing characterised by "long leaves drawn in supple, undulating strokes."[75] He argues that the way in which the leaf is often shown passing through an opening, as, for example, a

Photograph of Forsyth (wearing a hat) and other artists working on the Persian cartoon. Courtesy Manchester Art Gallery.

Print of the Persian panel, (the original cartoon is missing). Courtesy Salford Museum & Art Gallery.

hole in a rock, had magical significance in Persia. The rosettes at the centre of the leaf and the green and purple colours, which predominate in the borders, are typical of the period.

The undulating shape of the saz-leaf is found in much earlier Iznik ware where the decoration derives from manuscript illumination. This class of ware became known as "Golden Horn Ware" and dates from the 12th century. It is characterised by blue and white spiral decoration with comma shaped leaves. Also worked into the border are stylised tulips with three lobes. The tulip grew wild in Persia and this stylised representation was a common form on pottery and tiles. The flower was much admired by artists. In the Ottoman Empire "the eighteenth century is called the 'period of tulips'."[76] Alongside the leaves and tulips is the instantly recognisable carnation. It has a palmette form which Crane argued also had religious significance.

Finally, as with the other panels, there is a specific design at the base of the border. This appears to be a stylised form of the tree of life which has religious significance in many beliefs. This image is often depicted, as here, with tulip and saz-leaf.

A feature of Persian painting was the lack of a sense of true perspective. Forsyth seems to have consciously echoed this and the entire scene has the jewel-like quality of many Persian art works. The Persian contribution to many fields of art is reflected in the panel.

Persian music may be traced back to around 30 BC. Many distinctive Persian musical instruments are known. The woman in the bottom left corner of the scene is playing a "chang," an early form of harp.

The entire scene is set out on a carpet. In Crane's view "there are no better masters in the selection and treatment of natural forms in textile design than the Persians …."[77] Crane also extols the virtues of Persian embroidery and, on close inspection, one of the women may be seen working on a roll of material.

The curiously fashioned canopy lacks perspective. Similar shaped canopies may be seen in miniatures, for example, "Reception in a Garden," a miniature in the Topkapi Sarayi Museum, Istanbul. One of the figures appears to be either reading or writing a book, which is picked out in gold letters. This might be indicative of the Persian contribution to illuminated manuscripts or perhaps the strong tradition of Persian poetry. One of the most well-read Persian series of quatrains is Edward Fitzgerald's translation of the *Rubaiyat of Omar Khayyam*.

The male figure in the bottom right seems to be of particular importance. In Forsyth's image his turban is adorned with a special kind of feather, perhaps peacock, ostrich or a highly prized heron, which is set in a tulip-shaped ornament, worn on the right side and denotes a person of rank.

The detail of the vases is unclear but they appear to be bottle vases. The "Banquet Scene" features blue and white vases and Forsyth, in an identical manner, has three vases on his table.

The pot held by the man in the bottom right is blue and white with thin blue spiral bands winding around the vase. Blue on a silver ground was not uncommon and the Victoria and Albert Museum has examples of such ware. The outer two pots on the table appear to be blue and white. In connection with underglazed colours and the use of oxides of cobalt, Burton considered that "the potters of Persia and Syria had made extensive use of this mineral."[78] Burton states that the Chinese "not only derived the notion of painting in blue under-the-glaze from the Persians, but obtained their materials from the same source."[79]

Geza Fehervari describes in detail the blue and white wares, Kinbachi ware, of the 16th and 17th century Persian potters. These were finished in an alkaline tin glaze and were often used as drug pots (albarellos). They were also used as containers in the export of "candied fruits, spices, oils and perfumes to Europe."[80] Fehervari writes:

> "The invention of underglaze cobalt blue took place in Iran. The Kashan wares were simple stripes in a brilliant blue … [which] goes back to the thirteenth century."[81]

The Persian contribution to the potter's art was much more than lustreware. It is possible to trace pottery production back to the 8th century, which is where Forsyth began his story. The use of cobalt blue dates to the 9th century. In later centuries significant amounts of blue and white pottery were made at Kirman.

The other vases seem to have a lustrous sheen. The middle vase on the table has flecks of red in the Rhodian tradition.

The large canopy is very similar to the illustration in the "Banquet Scene" and may be a ceremonial umbrella used for shade. There also appear to be two vessels or water flasks attached to the pole which, along with swirling clouds, also appear in the "Banquet Scene". The figure seated under the awning is perhaps finishing the neck of a vase.

All the artists at Pilkington's appear to have been inspired by the motifs and colours used by Persian potters.[82] The panel was their homage to Persian ceramic art.

Examples of typical Persian inspired work by Pilkington's artists (not to scale).
Clockwise from top left:
12 x 6 inch tile
3 x 3 inch tile
Design for tile panel by Gordon Forsyth
Bowl signed by Joyce

THE GREEK PANEL – PATTERNS FOR THE CIVILISED WORLD

"You cannot understand literature written before 1900 without understanding the classics."[83]

Forsyth's panel "Greek 600 – 400 BC" is a reference to the "classical age" of Greece. It is an age that would have been well known to his generation as a study of the classics was essential for an educated man.

Pilkington's designs by Walter Crane and Lewis F. Day were in the classical style and the company reproduced classical scenes on many lustrewares. Crane, in *The Bases of Design*, described the pervading qualities of Greek design as "a simplicity of line," a "balance" and the possession of "a fundamental architectural feeling."

It is through its pottery and architecture that the Greek classical period is known to us today. The style of early Greek pottery, on which designs were repeated in geometric patterns often painted in slip, is known as 'proto-geometric.' By the 6th century BC the Athenian potteries had developed a style depicting the popular myths of the time. Pottery decoration reflected the stories of the gods and Homer's epic tales. Greek gods, unlike those in Persian or Egyptian art, took human form and for them, the Greeks perfected a new standard of figure painting.

Walter Crane, whose own art work often captured the human figure in classic Greek style, stated:

> "The Hellenic race, the Greeks, whose art has had, and still possesses, such an influence over that of the modern world, …treated the human figure as their chief element in decoration."[84]

By 500 BC proto-geometric ware was at its peak of production. The Greeks of this period did not use glaze. Vases were made in terracotta (unglazed pottery) of which Furnival says: "their vases in this material still form patterns for the civilized world."[85]

Furnival speculates on why the Greeks of this period did not use greater glaze colour effects. He finds it "incredible" to think that the Greeks of the fifth century BC who had trading contacts with Persia and Babylonia did not know of these effects. He concludes that the reason was simply that they could not make a more "effective" glaze than the "simple varnish and black enamel" they already had. Other theories consider that the use of glazes then available would not have been technically compatible with the style of decoration and might have obscured the sharp lines needed for it.

The Greeks of the classical Attic period used a black or matt red slip over orange or red clay and scratched lines into the slip to enhance the detail. The firing process changed the slip into a lustrous finish. Various reversals of this colour combination including a white slip were used. Many authorities considered that the figurative decoration of pottery declined after 400 BC.

In addition to their decorative style the Greeks also produced pottery in styles which were functional, as for example: the amphora for holding and storing water, oil or wine; the hydria for carrying water; the krater for mixing; the kylix for pouring wine and other vessels for drinking. Arthur Lane, in his classic work on Greek pottery, wrote that the Greeks reconciled "the threefold demands of utility, of form, and of decoration."[86]

Pilkington's modelled several shapes upon Greek forms. In particular, their lustre catalogue illustrated a magnificent hydria. The Pilkington's "lady" artists, as they were known, specialised in small box and lidded forms akin to the Greek "Pyxis" shape. John Chambers is said to have been responsible for introducing Greek shapes into the Pilkington's range though all the artists would have known of them. One of Chambers' shapes is based on the kylix and Pilkington's produced its Greek shapes in both lustre and matt glazes.

A lustre hydria illustrated in a Pilkington's pottery catalogue.

The achievement of Greek culture in other fields, in philosophy, mathematics, architecture, verse and seafaring is symbolised in the cartoon. The panel is unusual in that the same theme forms both the external border and the base of the panel. Owen Jones illustrates a variety of Greek ornamental styles, some of which may be found in this panel.

It became the practice in the Attic period for artists to sign their work, something Pilkington's also encouraged. Exekias was the principal potter of the Attic period and is thought to have been working in Athens about 530 BC. The work at the base of the panel and forming the outer border is taken from a krater, or drinking cup[87], signed by Exekias. Many Greek vase decorations were in a narrative style. This subject is that of Dionysus, the god of wine, sailing amongst a shoal of dolphins. The mast of the ship supports a grapevine, which on the krater fills the bowl. On the panel, Forsyth has allowed the vine to fill the entire border. The colour of the Exekias krater is a coral red which Forsyth has also used. The comparison between that and a similar design by Forsyth (Cross p.45) confirms that the image of Dionysus was known by Pilkington's in 1906. Burton and Forsyth may have used this to ensure a stronger connection with the Greek potter's art.

Forsyth's signature on the cartoon.

The Sea Maiden, a vase designed by Walter Crane and decorated by Pilkington's artists. Courtesy Towneley Hall Museum and Art Gallery, Burnley.

The representation of the prow on the ship is also relevant to Pilkington's. Walter Crane executed several designs for the company of which one, the Sea Maiden, is well known. Dionysus was born from the union of Semele and Zeus who had taken the form of a swan. In the cartoon the two winged figures which support the banner may be stylised forms of winged Greek gods, perhaps the Erotes, the youthful gods of love. Greek lyric song links the Erotes and Dionysus.

The inner border on the cartoon is more conventional and is similar to those illustrated by Owen Jones. The Greek key and the "egg and dart" designs might have been taken from Jones or indeed any other work of the time on Greek ornament. Pilkington's produced various border

The sketch for the Greek panel. Courtesy National Museums Liverpool.

Proof of the Lancaster Print of the Greek panel. Courtesy of the Rare Book Archive, Lancaster University.

The Greek cartoon. Courtesy Salford Museum & Art Gallery.

infills based on these and other Greek designs. Their 1900 pattern book contains examples of the key and anthemion designs. Lewis F. Day designed tiles for Pilkington's, to be used in a frieze or dado, as early as 1897 and for later exhibitions.

Of all the panels the Greek varies most markedly from the scale drawing which was probably never meant to be more than a sketch. The border appears hastily drawn with a free flowing vine and typical Greek ornaments across the top. The vine on the cartoon is much more stylised and forms a rectangular border. Dionysus has also been added, the figure of Athena has been changed and two youths have been added to hold the banner showing the dates.

The Lancaster print for the Greek panel appears to have been made before the cartoon was finalised as there are significant changes, as for example, in the figure of Athena and the statue of Nike. The main change compared with the scale drawing is the depiction of the intended border. It may well be that this print was a representation of the original cartoon that was changed following Bosanquet's comments.

The Liverpool scale drawing for this panel is entitled "Greek: presentation of pot of oil to Olympic Victor." Forsyth seems genuinely appreciative of the help of the Liverpool authorities classics expert, Professor Bosanquet. In a letter dated 18th December 1914 he indicates to Dr. Clubb that he will "embody" Professor Bosanquet's suggestions into the finished work and states that "we are very much indebted to Professor Bosanquet for the trouble he has taken and the valuable help he has given in connection with the work."

Along with this letter is a typewritten note from Professor Bosanquet suggesting several changes to the scale drawing which Forsyth has incorporated. He removes the helmet from the central figure and changes the hairstyle, alters facial characteristics to reflect a more "Greek" appearance and adjusts the toga of the youth holding the bridle. Bosanquet suggests that Forsyth examine the Parthenon frieze to gain an idea of the style. The vase being presented should, Bosanquet says, be a Panathenaic amphora [though it appears to be a hydria in both the scale drawing and the final cartoon]. Finally, it is observed that in the cartoon "the spears have the appearance of having lashings to hold the spearhead. This is not correct, as the spearhead was always socketed."

The subject of the panel is self-evident from the title. The classic Panathenaic amphora is a very large container and it is no wonder that the small boys are struggling with it. An amphora of this kind was awarded to the winners of events at the Panathenaic Games in Athens. The winner astride a horse may have been chosen after Forsyth took Bosanquet's advice to study the decoration of the Parthenon frieze. Contestants in the games would traditionally compete naked though Forsyth, perhaps for reasons of Edwardian sensibilities, does not carry this theme too far. Vases with decoration depicting a presentation or scenes from the games are common.

The Parthenon (the temple of the maiden) is said to have been constructed in 480 BC. It is seen in the background of the panel. Within was an enormous statue of Athena. The temple was constructed on the order of Pericles who also commissioned other buildings including a temple to Nike.

The goddess of War (and of Athens), Athena, is the dominant figure with spear and shield. According to myth, she had a contest with Poseidon, god of the sea, to decide who was to be the ruler of Attica (the land around Athens) and this traditional presentation is in her honour. She is sometimes depicted holding a spear, as here, or holding a statue of Nike who represents victory and beauty and appears here as a winged figure on a column. Interestingly, there are other discernible differences between the initial scale drawing which indicates that Bosanquet may have suggested other changes. There is no figure of Nike in the original scale drawing and in the cartoon the column replaces a pole.

In the scale drawing, which is a traditional representation, Athena wears a helmet surmounted by a sphinx. Her breastplate depicts the face of Medusa, another figure from Greek mythology. The sea and ship in the lower part of the panel is a reference to Greek seafaring skills and the many sailing ships they built. The similarity of Greek and Roman ornament is emphasised in the next panel.

This image of the base of the Greek cartoon has been digitally repaired and is taken from a photograph of the actual panel.

The sketch for the Roman panel. Courtesy National Museums Liverpool.

THE ROMAN PANEL – POTTERY OF CONQUEST

If the Persian panel was a work of which Burton and Forsyth seemed especially proud because of its artistic merit, the Roman panel seems to be a work which had a personal connection. In a letter to Dr. Clubb[88] in December 1914 Forsyth stated:

> "The central idea of this panel is the building of the Roman kilns at Holt near Chester where extensive excavations were made by Mr. Arthur Acton and Mr. Burton and actual models of these kilns have been made at the works here.
>
> Wherever the Romans went as conquerors they took the craft of the potter, thus greatly helping forward the ceramic art in manufacture and artistic accomplishment e.g. the effect on British pottery.
>
> The borders of the panel are based on figures and ornaments which usually surround Arretine and Samian bowls. Loeb collection and Walters Roman Pottery in the British Museum."

Forsyth's letter refers to the extensive excavations by Arthur Acton[89] of Roman kilns at Holt in Denbighshire, about 7 miles from Chester on the River Dee. Joseph Burton was consulted because he was "an acknowledged authority on the subject." Neither the models of the kilns nor any family records of this involvement have been found.

Roman kilns are found all over the Roman empire. Both Burtons were aware of the importance and extent of Roman pottery production in Britain. Roman kilns varied in their complexity, simple kilns were rebuilt after each firing. However, the kilns at Holt were permanent and much more sophisticated.

The kiln depicted in the cartoon is presumably the type that was modelled at Pilkington's. Grimes (who presented Acton's work) says that "an attempt was made to build solid structures by forming an outer casing of sandstone masonry against the sides of the pit, within which the kiln proper was built of tiles ... no attempt was made at coursing the masonry except where it was exposed to view on the large bastion-like cheeks which flanked the approach to the fire-hole."[90]

The works depot at Holt has many features unique among Roman potteries in Britain. It was exceptionally extensive occupying about 20 acres, and comprised domestic buildings: workmen's barrack-blocks, a bath building, a dwelling house as well as industrial buildings: two sets of workshops, a drying shed, a double flue kiln, the main kiln plant and the clay pits. The main plant, 136 feet long and 58.5 feet wide at its greatest width, consisted of a battery of six tile and pottery kilns.

We can deduce, from Acton's papers, that Joseph Burton's professional opinion was sought to help explain what was being uncovered. Acton's comment that Joseph Burton was an acknowledged authority on

Detail from the Roman cartoon.

the subject continued by noting that Burton agreed "that the Holt kilns differ very little from modern kilns, of similar type, ... they were constructed to carry the heat as efficiently as possible to the outside of the kiln, a very necessary arrangement if good firing is to result."

Forsyth refers to Arretine ware, which was originally made in Arretium, the modern Arezzo, in northern Italy, during the 1st century AD. Both Arretine and Samian ware were prized above other types of pottery in their time and were used as tableware; it has been found in all parts of the Roman Empire. Mayer described Arretine

Proof of the Lancaster Print of the Roman panel. Courtesy of the Rare Book Archive, Lancaster University.

56

The Roman cartoon. The base is badly damaged and distortion due to the warped canvas has caused the scaffolding poles to appear rippled. Courtesy Salford Museum & Art Gallery.

ware as "a higher class of ware, darker in tone, with ornaments better moulded, and more carefully finished, but very similar to [Samian ware] at a casual glance."[91] Samian pottery is so called because it was produced on the Greek island of Samos. It is characterised by being a rich red brown in colour and is often decorated with classical scenes. It was also decorated with various flora, fauna and hunting scenes.

The scene on this panel is set in the 2nd century AD, regarded as the best period for Samian ware. After the Roman invasion of Britain there was a need to begin local production because importing pottery would have been expensive. The Romans originally brought their own craftsmen and so began not only a new pottery production process but also a transfer of skills to British potters. This was the "effect" upon British pottery to which Forsyth referred.

The pottery was made of earthenware and was prone to damage, hence the need for a constant supply. The ware was moulded or thrown. The pottery was needed for storage, for the preparation of food and for carrying water. Best known is the amphora, a two-handled jar. Different styles of amphorae are known; some end in a lower body point and others have an extended neck. By coincidence a short article on Samian ware appeared in *The Pottery Gazette*[92] immediately after a report of William Burton's lecture to the Society of Arts entitled "The Palette of the Potter."

Mayer and many others held that the Greeks influenced much of Roman pottery. In particular, three links are identified: Roman clays, like those of Greece, were rich in red iron oxide, work was impressed with the name of the maker or workshop owner and Roman pottery also showed a preference for relief decoration.[93]

Furnival's appreciation of the contribution of the Romans to the potter's art concentrates on mosaic work. Examples of Pompeian mosaic may be found in the Grosvenor Museum, Chester, which would have been known to Joseph Burton.

The lower portion of the cartoon is badly damaged. More information may be gleaned from the photograph at Liverpool Museum and the Lancaster print. The main border is classical in style with acanthus leaves in each corner in the style illustrated by Owen Jones. It has not been possible to ascertain the significance of the frieze beneath the main image. Forsyth described it as "based on figures and ornaments which usually surround Arretine and Samian bowls" but without further explanation.

Catherine Johns provides a detailed account of Arretine and Samian pottery in her short account of the pieces at the British Museum.[94] One vase in particular is relevant to our study. A vessel is illustrated "decorated in Claudian style." The decoration around the rim is similar to Forsyth's border. Also depicted on the cartoon border are two slim amphorae which serve to remind us of the pervasion of Roman pottery production.

Richard Burns, Curator at Bury Art Gallery and Museum in Greater Manchester, has speculated that the male figure might be related to the story of Vertumnus who disguised himself as a herdsman to woo Pomona. The scene also contains a figure that might be Pan who was often accompanied by Bacchus in Roman imagery. (The small figure on the column might be a representation of Bacchus offering grapes.)

The Liverpool scale drawing for the Roman panel has no border and is only a rudimentary sketch. Differences between it, the Lancaster print and the finished cartoon are clear. In particular, the design of the imperial standard has changed twice and the entrance to the kiln is more detailed and similar to illustrations in Acton's papers. Perhaps these changes were made in response to requests from the museum authorities.

A laurel wreath, signifying victory, surrounds the entire panel; it is a typical Roman motif and appropriate for the panel's main subject.

The imagery in the central panel is more readily understood. Chester's importance as a Roman town is well documented. Furnival describes "Deva (Chester)" as "this central stronghold, upon which five Roman roads converged, [which] became a flourishing town."[95]

The Roman invasion of Britain in 43 AD, leading to its later conquest, necessitated the building of a network of forts. At Chester the main difficulty for the occupying force was the opposition of native tribes in Wales which was heavily exploited by the Romans for its gold deposits. It was not until 78 AD that Wales was fully occupied.

The Roman Legion based at Chester was Legio XX (the Twentieth) with the motto Valeria Victrix (Valiant and Victorious). This legion is first documented in Britain in Colchester in 43 AD and was gradually moved further north until it had arrived in Chester by 88 AD. Its title appears to have come from its victory over the Boadicean rebels in 60/61 AD. The Romans remained in Deva until 383 AD, by which time the silting up of the River Dee led to the abandonment of the town.

From their arrival in Deva onwards the Romans would have needed a steady supply of bricks, tiles and pottery. This need would have been supplied by the pottery which they set up at Holt. Pottery would have been transported to Chester along the River Dee.

In the cartoon we can see labourers carrying heavy blocks to supply the workmen building the kiln. The imperial standard clearly identifies the legion "LEG XX VV" as does the inscription above the circular arch forming the entrance to the kiln and the relief moulding of a boar which was the legion's symbol.

The lower detail of the cartoon depicts the labourers crossing a perilous looking plank. It is placed across a boat with a rudder or tiller which seems far too large for the young boy sitting there. It is likely that the stone is being offloaded from a boat anchored alongside in the River Dee.

An altar stone at Deva was dedicated to several of the Roman and Greek gods, one of whom was the goddess Fortuna. The carving on the altar stone is that of a rudder which is a symbol of life's course set by Fortuna.

The Roman panel is the last of the tile panels that were installed.

SAMIAN WARE.

FRAGMENTS of a Roman bowl in red Samian ware were found last month upon the site of the Roman Camp at Gelligaer, South Wales. These fragments were in an extremely decayed condition, but they have been satisfactorily hardened, and were found to make up about two-thirds of the vessel. The bowl has been successfully reconstructed in Cardiff Museum, some of the missing portions being supplied by plaster casts taken from the existing parts. It is of the beautiful red pottery known as Samian ware and is seven inches in diameter. The decoration is in low relief, and depicts a forest scene. There are trees of highly conventional character, upon the boughs of which are birds, while other birds may be noticed on the ground below. Sundry beasts, amongst them a lion and a hart, are also conspicuous. Samian ware was to the Romans what porcelain is to us. It seems to have been in general use, for it is rare to find it absent from a Roman site. Many fragments have been found during the excavations which have taken place at Cardiff Castle during the last three years.

Extract from *The Pottery Gazette*, 1st November 1900.

THE PANELS THAT NEVER HAPPENED

THE ITALIAN PANEL – FORMS SO WONDROUS FAIR

Forsyth and Burton clearly felt that the other panels were relevant to the history of pottery and for this reason this publication also concerns itself with their story.

The Italian cartoon is not complete and no corresponding sketch exists at Liverpool.

In 1906 W. Burton said: "Our latest development has been the production of a Lancastrian lustre pottery. It is to cover the whole range of lustre effects, and is like the old Hispano-Moresque and Persian lustre."[96]

Following an earlier paper by William De Morgan,[97] Burton's lecture to the Society of Arts was also reprinted in *The Pottery Gazette*. Burton covered the entire field of lustre pottery from ancient Persia to modern factories.

In the tradition of De Morgan and Burton, Forsyth also delivered a lecture "Lustred pottery: ancient and modern"[98] reported in *The Pottery Gazette*. Forsyth describes how, whilst the lustre process was first used in Egypt, it was the Persian potters who brought it to "perfection before the thirteenth century." This lustre process was carried to Spain where a copper lustre was introduced which toned down the silver and produced a quieter lustre. This ware is known as Hispano-Moresque and combined traditional lustre designs with heraldic devices, often of important families.

Spanish pottery was imported into Italy via the island of Majorca; the generic term majolica is used for this kind of ware. Majolica was characterised by a white glaze caused by the presence of tin oxide. Later developments in tin glazes extended the range of colours to the full palette. Initially objects were dipped to obtain a white covering and later, decorated, dried and fired. Tin enamel provided an impervious surface on which the decorator could exercise his skills. Forsyth's statement, "there was no doubt that the lustres of the Hispano-Moresque potters inspired the Italian craftsmen," brings us to the subjects of the tile panel itself.

Little can be said about the incomplete border. The cartoon itself is in such a friable condition that it was not advisable to force the canvas open to study it. The design appears to contain a winged man and part of a horse, possibly a centaur, images typical of Italian renaissance motifs.

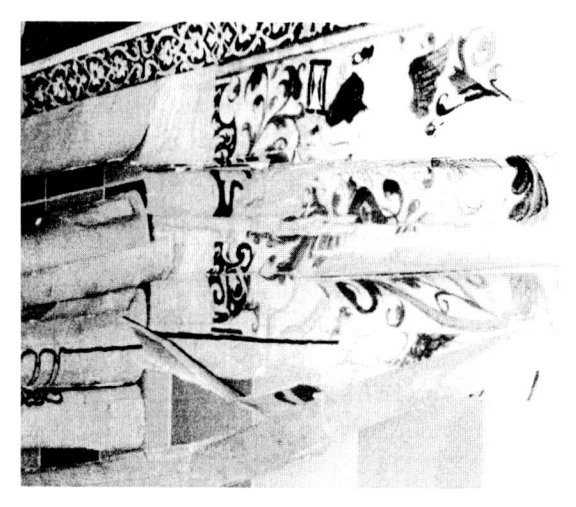

The base of the cartoon is badly damaged; in this digitally enhanced image a winged figure can just be seen.

At the top of the panels two putti draw the eye to the inscriptions on the flowing rib-

Detail from the Italian cartoon.

The Italian cartoon. Courtesy Salford Museum & Art Gallery.

bon, "LVCA DELLA ROBBIA MAESTRO GIORGIO", and the medallion encircled by a laurel wreath, "FAENZA CAFFAGGIOLO DIRVTA GVBBIO"; these tell the story of Italian pottery. The scene is set in a market place. The putti, a common image in Italian art during the 15th – 17th centuries, are related to the Greek Eros and the Roman Cupid. The idea may have been inspired by the relief plaques on many Italian buildings of this period, for example, those modelled by della Robbia on the walls of the Hospital of the Innocents in Florence. The hospital has arches and classical columns similar to those in Forsyth's image. The colour of the lettered panel may have been chosen to reflect the "berettino" style (see below).

Forsyth's panel reflects the imagery used in the pottery of the Renaissance (1400-1550). Pottery made in Florence during this period was influenced by Spanish ware and representations on pharmacy vessels included designs of animals, particularly birds and lions. The general term for such ware was "orvieto" named after the town where large quantities of this pottery have been found. The decorative influence was clearly Spanish.

Faenza was famous in the Renaissance for its ceramic production. Many of its artists worked throughout Europe, which further enhanced its reputation. In particular, it was noted for its production of majolica. Furnival dates its earliest pottery production to 1393. In common with several Italian towns, pottery here was patronised by powerful families, in Faenza by the Manfredi family. The various motifs of this family were "lions rampant, greyhounds, birds and fleurs-de-lys, all painted using a thick blue pigment."[99] Another style associated with the town is "berettino," blue decoration over a grey blue ground.

A general style of decoration known as Istoriato Majolica (history paintings) was also developed. Large ceramic forms, plates or chargers, were decorated with biblical or classical scenes often copying the Italian masters. Faenza was a centre of such work. The town's reputation was at its peak in the 15th century; production continued until the end of the 16th century with "bianchi di Faenza," a lightly decorated white ware. Commemorative ware also featured strongly.

Lustre pottery was made between 1490 and 1545 at Deruta (DIRVTA) in a style similar to Faenza. Prior to this, tin glazed ware had been made. This school of painters favoured a warm yellow and blue palate. The decoration was created by sgraffito. In a similar way to the Roman process, cuts in the clay contain the glaze within its sunken borders. (Pilkington's, especially W.S. Mycock, utilised a sgraffito style.) Ware from Deruta is lavishly decorated and can be very large in size. Pilkington's exhibition pieces are often presented on a similar large scale.

Caffaggiolo near Florence was another centre of potting. The arms of the Medici family often appear on its ware and the influence of Italian artists, for example Botticelli and Donatello, is noticeable. A peacock feather style of ornament was developed here and their palette favoured rich blues and dark cherry reds. Istoriato ware was also made in Caffaggiolo.

Luca della Robbia (1397-1482) was a sculptor from Florence who made terracotta bas-relief, using the tin glazing technique in a slightly different way, for architectural adornment. Instead of over-painting with oxides, he added the oxides to the tin glaze and made solid coloured glazes. His techniques influenced decoration and style. The bas-relief was much imitated by the English company Della Robia.[100] Furnival states that della Robbia's fame "rests largely also upon his bronzes and his marble sculptures."[101]

Maestro Giorgio Andreoli, "Maestro Giorgio," was a native of Lombardy and moved to Gubbio in 1498. The finest production of pottery was in the first quarter of the sixteenth century. They were rich in lustres, often heavily cut to reflect the colours; most famous were gold and ruby lustres, which seem to be shown in the cartoon. Such was his skill that he also decorated for workshops besides his own. He was so important that he was exempted from paying taxes and was granted citizenship.

Arthur Veel Rose provided a very detailed account concerning Maestro Giorgio. Veel Rose was the self-titled "pottery expert" of Tiffany's in New York. His report was originally published in *The American Pottery Gazette*.[102] He illustrated his report with some excellent examples of ruby and gold lustre in the Hispano-Moresque style. He also featured pottery designed by Walter Crane and Lewis F. Day.

Much of Pilkington's pottery depicts the Hispano-Moresque style. In the Mycock Archive at Salford Museum and Art Gallery there is a folder devoted to "heraldic" designs and several photographs of Hispano-Moresque ware. Forsyth wrote of this ware that "there was no doubt" that the Hispano-Moresque potters (of Spain) inspired Italian craftsmen. Noel Riley illustrates a majolica tile with a rampant lion design in a tin glaze and dated 1480.

A.J. Cross has observed that Pilkington's often mixed different styles; this heraldic device on a classic Greek pyxis or pill box is a good example.

The heraldic influence is particularly strong on Pilkington's lustre tiles.

Anabella Wake,[103] of Adelaide, South Australia, hosts a website illustrating Renaissance costume. She has explained the meaning of the images along with some speculation:

"Although it is a re-drawing, and the modern influence is very noticeable, there is no doubt that the drawing of the woman in the far right of the scene is based upon the images by Domenico Ghirlandaio of a woman seen in some of the frescos of the Cappella Tornabuoni, Santa Maria Novella, Florence, and as such can be dated squarely in to the 1580s.

The woman is thought to be Giovanna degli Albizzi, who married Lorenzo Tornabuoni. Her likeness can be seen in several frescos and one panel painting. The frescos are from the series "Stories of the Virgin" - specifically "Birth of Mary", and "Visitation." The image in "Visitation" is also the same image that appears in the panel painting of Giovanna Tornabuoni dated 1488, the year in which she died. I believe this to be the image used as inspiration for your tile panel art work. The hair style she wears in your image is different. It is down, rather than up. It is called a *"coazzone"* and can be seen in Giovanna's image in "Birth of Mary." She wears a shift (*camisa*), underdress (*cotta* in summer and *gamurra* in winter) and over-dress (*giornea*).

Going from right to left, the next image in your art work is of a man who is partly hidden. From what I can see, he appears to be wearing the *cappucio* - a stuffed roll hat which evolved from a hood worn rolled up. The next man along is also wearing one, this time with dagged *fogia* (the bits sticking out at the top of the hat). The man further left is more problematical because it is harder to see him clearly, but I think it to be a less well drawn depiction of a *cappucio*. The *cappuccio* was seen from late 14th century (about 1390) right through to approximately 1470.

The first man appears to be wearing a short over-gown which was quite often lined with fur (*giornea*), probably worn over a close-fitting doublet (*farsetto*). The clothing of the next two men appears to be inspired by other styles. The man in the yellow is wearing a *farsetto* and *calze* (hose) with cape, typical for the younger men of the 1490s, but the one next to him is odd - he is either wearing a short *cioppa* (a type of over-gown) belted around the waist, or a long-skirted doublet of some kind, and boots (*stivali*).

The remaining figures are too indistinct to for me to comment on them confidently, except to say that from what little I can see, these women appear to be wearing similar, if less ornate, clothing to Giovanna."

PANELS 2 AND 9 - THE EGYPTIAN AND THE EARLY ENGLISH

Although sketches were known to have been produced for these panels, artwork has never been found. The Egyptian panel would have been particularly appropriate because of the proximity of the Egyptian room in the museum.

Furnival devotes several pages to the contribution of Egypt to the potter's art. Owen Jones would have provided ample source material for borders. W. Burton in his 1907 lecture talked of the oldest of lustres which were discovered in Egypt. In particular, Burton admired the use of gold in Egyptian ornament. A fascination with Egyptian motifs, for example, the pyramid and the sphinx, was also fashionable around 1912 and Burton would also be aware of the ways in which Wedgwood echoed the Egyptian style, for example, in black basalt.

The Early English panel is described as "English potters of the 17th and 18th century (Toft, Wedgwood)"[104] and was to have contained references to their pottery. The Wedgwood aspect of this work would have appealed to Burton who spent five years at that factory before joining Pilkington's. The reference to Toft would immediately cause any student of pottery to think of slipware. A slip is diluted clay which has the consistency of cream. Forsyth considered the use of slip in his own book on the potter's craft. He noted that the "best way" to apply it is "as icing might be applied to a cake." He notes that only simple patterns are possible "but that is the great charm of the process ... brought to a high degree of perfection in the middle of the seventeenth century."[105] He states that the Staffordshire potters, Thomas and Ralf Toft, were the most noted for this type of decoration but that other potters, for example in Kent, produced excellent ware. He found it entirely "natural" that slip decoration would be the first method used by potters.

Burton's connection with Wedgwood is well known, but that was not a reason to include the company on the proposed cartoon. Geoffrey Godden states that "...it is quite impossible to prepare a comprehensive work on British pottery without including a section on Josiah Wedgwood and the firm founded by this master potter."[106]

Wedgwood's reputation was based on his standards of perfection, his designs and his decoration. He was also adept at promoting his own company and established London showrooms to circumvent the restrictions of selling at the time.

As with the Egyptian panel, there is no hint as to what was contained in the image.

Time had run out, Forsyth had taken up war service, fashions had changed and the impetus was lost.

**Pilkington's used this sphinx to advertise their faience ware.
Courtesy Salford Museum & Art Gallery.**

THE LIVERPOOL PANELS - CONNECTIONS WITH THE POTTER'S CRAFT

The tile panels featuring Liverpool and its connections to the sea and the potter's craft were never commissioned. Forsyth's scale drawings for the suggested panels are annotated:

> "Large panel Liverpool and its connections with the potter's Craft. Small panel "the Liverpool Bowl". Panels on the opposite side to go with this might be Modern manufacture and small panel showing fritting of glaze."[107]

Both Forsyth and William Burton were well aware of the history of Liverpool and its pottery connections. Burton summarised the Liverpool connection in his book, *Porcelain, A Sketch of its Nature Art and Manufacture* and in his work on Wedgwood.[108,109]

The present museum staff explained the iconography as follows:

> "The panel consists of two sections. One section depicts the figure of Britannia possibly symbolising the Liverpool gateway to the British Empire. She appears to be receiving gifts from a group of gentlemen. The writing accompanying the panel explains that the image shows Liverpool and its connections with the potter's crafts. In the foreground two cherubs are seated either side of a cartouche depicting a possible version of a Liver bird.
>
> The second section of the panel depicts four cherubs encircling what is probably a ship bowl. The inclusion of a ship in the bottom left-hand corner indicates Liverpool's connection with ship bowls. The writing accompanying the panel explains it was intended to be the Liverpool bowl.
>
> After about 1700, it became common to share a bowl of punch rather than to drink from the same cup. The punch was ladled out into individual glasses. If you were a Liverpool merchant or shipmaster wanting to drink to the success of your ship's latest voyage, a local pottery would make a bowl decorated with your ship. These ship bowls would have been made from ceramic bodies including porcelain, delftware, pearlware or creamware."

The staff also point out that not all the costumes are authentic for the 18th century, though there is a lack of detail in the image. Some of the other characters wear costume which might be 16th century. They continue:

> "Since 1672, Britannia has been anthropomorphised into a woman wearing a helmet and carrying a shield and trident. It is a symbol that blends the concepts of empire, militarism and economics. Liverpool played a prominent role as a provincial port city. It was also the leading transatlantic port in Europe from the 18th until the early 20th century."

Example of a Liverpool bowl. Courtesy National Museums Liverpool.

The image of the Liver bird seems at first glance to differ slightly from a more modern representation. The Liver bird has changed forms many times.[110] Its modern prominence and almost instantaneous connection with Liverpool derives from the two birds placed on the waterfront offices of the Royal Liver Friendly Society in 1911. This timing seems particularly apt for the tile panels. The city's connection

The Liverpool sketch, intended for the wall alongside the stairway. Courtesy National Museums Liverpool.

with the bird dates back to 1352 with the first surviving impression of the corporate seal. Even before this there are possible connections in 1207. The bird has metamorphosed from eagle to cormorant, to a dove and then to the modern image of today. The name Liver is said to be a corruption of a Dutch word for bird, which conveniently fitted phonetically with Liverpool.

W. Burton cited Mayer's history, which featured numerous illustrations of bowls decorated with sailing ships, in his book on Wedgwood. Liverpool Museum has many fine examples of these "blue and white" ceramics.

Although Forsyth's suggestion for the scheme focused on pottery, he will have been aware of Liverpool's connection with tiles. Julian Barnard[111] lists Liverpool amongst the three English centres of tile production in the 18th century (along with London and Bristol). Barnard explains how the first mechanical process to decorate tiles involved the use of transfer-printing and was developed by Sadler and Green in Liverpool. This process could produce up to 1200 tiles a day. This soon led to the Wedgwood connection. Josiah Wedgwood was sending "crates of biscuit fired pots to Liverpool from Burslem for decoration."[112] Sadler's work was not just about producing volume. Barnard makes the point that the quality and freshness of design was a significant factor in the success of the ware. Tile production was still a laborious business in the 18th century as tile bodies were made, cut and shaped by hand. This changed in the mid-19th century with the work of Herbert Minton (1793 – 1858) who revolutionised production by enabling tile bodies to be made as speedily as Sadler could decorate them.

Liverpool as a city was well endowed with tiled buildings[113] (including the Lister Drive Baths). Noel Riley writes:

> "The City of Liverpool, well placed for exporting to America and the West Indies, became the most prolific centre of delftware tile production during the 18th century. The first factory was set up in Lord Street in 1710 by Richard Holt, with workmen from Southwark. A contemporary newspaper announcement affirmed its intention to produce 'all sorts of fine and painted pots and other vessels and tiles in imitation of China both for Inland and Outland trade'…".[114]

This makes it clear that tiles were produced from the outset and that export was a major consideration. Several other factories were set up in Liverpool during the 18th century, many of them producing tiles, although detailed evidence is scant.

In any work concerned with Liverpool and pottery it would be remiss not to mention the Della Robbia pottery established in Birkenhead in 1893. Della Robbia might even have been the museum's first thought for executing the work had the factory not ceased production in 1906. Myra Brown illustrates two stunning Della Robbia panels which indicate that their artists were most capable.[115]

The Tiles and Architectural Society (TACS) featured what has been described as "Liverpool's Last Pottery Manufacturer" in a *Glazed Expressions* publication[116] concerned with the Swan Tile Works in Liverpool. Little is known about the tile works although production appears to have been variable and not up to the demands of a commission like the one proposed for the museum.

The final connection is to the site of the museum itself, built adjacent to one of the early Liverpool potteries on Shaw's Brow.[117]

In conclusion, the reason why the museum was favourably disposed to the Liverpool panels is not hard to find. However, why they were never commissioned is unknown. The museum kept the artwork and it may be that the authorities wished to wait until the main installation was completed. As the war continued they probably found themselves overtaken by costs and changes in attitudes.

THE PREHISTORIC PANEL - "CLAY CREATED THE POTTER"

In a letter dated 26th January 1914 Mr. Entwistle of Liverpool Museum listed the various tile panels it was hoped to commission. The first of these he calls "the prehistoric period". On 4th February 1914 Pilkington's Secretary Edwin Wardle sent a short note to Dr. Clubb to advise that "the two further designs of the Neolithic or Bronze Age, and the groups of 17th and 18th century potters are now ready for your inspection, and we should be pleased to learn if it would be convenient to you for Mr. Forsyth to wait on you with them on Friday next …". An even briefer note finally arranged a meeting on the 10th for Mr. Forsyth to bring both designs.

This cartoon is the most damaged. It has been squashed at some time which accounts for the ripple effect that is still clearly visible. The top of the cartoon has broken up and to a considerable extent the digital recreation is flawed. The border itself is the least complete of all the panels.

There is an argument for putting this panel first in this account. The panel signified the first production of pottery. It was decided to put it last for two reasons. Firstly, Burton himself felt this period was less to do with the potter's art and more to do with the utility that pottery offered. Secondly, because little is known about the subject it is open to greater speculation than the other panels.

Even the title, the prehistoric period, is vague. The references above to the Neolithic and Bronze Age complicate matters. It is not known what "age" Forsyth intended. There is a difference between Neolithic and Bronze Age pottery not just of time but of style.

In 1897 William Burton wrote:

> "Of all the crafts practised by man that of the potter is among the most ancient and the most universal. For spinning or weaving, for working in metals, in wood, or in bone, some intricate or troublesome preparation of natural material is required; but the prime material of the potter – clay – lies ready to hand in almost every region of the earth's surface, needing so little preparation to fit it for use, and so rapidly manifesting its power of taking and retaining the shape of any object squeezed into it, that we may almost say: "Clay created the potter." As to the invention of pottery, that need not delay us a moment; a device so obvious as the making of the simplest form of pottery is within the scope of a child, given the material; and every tribe, or race of men inhabiting a district where clay was to be found would as naturally become potters as the dwellers by lake or stream became fishermen, or people living by the sea became navigators. All the primitive races of ancient or modern times have not only practised the potter's craft, but have practised it in the same rude and elementary way. A glance at the collections of primitive pottery in any good museum will reveal the whole extent of such a potter's craft. Vessels of rude but not unpleasing shape, scooped out from a ball of clay, or patiently built up piece by piece as some birds build their nests; softened into shape by pliant fingers or simplest tools, and then hardened by prolonged drying in the sun; such is, in brief, the potter's craft in its simplest form – the starting point from which all the world's work in clay has grown."[118]

Ceramic art (*keramos* is the Greek word for clay), Burton stresses, is to do with the "decoration" of ware and this would include "modelling, carving, incising and inlaying."

Furnival states that the origin of decorative ceramic art is "lost in the mists of antiquity." He echoes Burton's point by saying that where clay deposits are rare then the use of ceramic products is subservient.

Modern studies date the appearance of ceramics to the seventh millennium BC but for the purposes of this particular tile panel there are a few clues as to what Forsyth had in mind.

The border itself is only partially sketched. If we "look closely," as the Chinese proverb has it, we may gain some knowledge, although this is highly speculative. The ornamental style of the border is relatively simple and a faint outline of a snake or worm-like creature may be seen. There is also the faint outline of a design with diagonal bands running left to right in a square.

More study may reveal the significance of this border but the one thing that can be stated is that it depicts a "pattern." Patterns can also be seen on the pottery and the dress and headwear of the figures in the main panel. Lewis F. Day was Pilkington's most celebrated early designer. His book *Pattern Design*, published in 1903, describes pattern "as ornament and especially ornament in repetition"[119] and "the natural outgrowth of repetition." Day points out that any "primitive workmanship produces pattern. To plait, to net, to weave, or in any way mechanically to make, is to produce pattern".[120] Pattern is an artistic intent.

Day argues that the "simplest" of all patterns is the stripe but that the limits of the stripe are soon reached and might be taken further, for example, by a zigzag. He considers that the "primitive weaver" must have built up the lattice and chequered patterns. From these he traces the evolution of pattern through groups of squares to more complex repeats and frets and so on. More complicated variations that cut across a simple lattice produce a triangle which may give way to an octagon, a circle and eventually the ogee shape.

The people represented in the panel are clearly living in a community which appears relatively advanced and certainly the woman's dress has gone beyond mere animal skins. The clothing is deliberately patterned in quite an intricate manner.[121]

The border of the Prehistoric cartoon has been digitally enhanced to illustrate the very faint outlines of the pattern design.

The Prehistoric cartoon. Courtesy Salford Museum & Art Gallery.

Burton referred to the methods of primitive pottery as involving ware "patiently built up piece by piece."

Several years after he painted the tile panels Forsyth wrote *Art and Craft of the Potter*. In it he speculates on the "most primitive" methods of making pottery. These might be the way a piece of clay was stamped accidentally by an animal's foot, or the way a piece of clay was wrapped around a stone to make a simple bowl shape. Forsyth describes a method called "coiling" as one of the most primitive modes of production. He notes that it is still practised by Pueblo Mexican Indians[122] "who have never known of the existence of a 'throwing wheel'. They manage, however, to make beautiful shapes; with a surface comparable to that turned on a throwing wheel and finished on a turning lathe."[123]

In the pot shown below a primitive pattern of repeated diagonals or triangles is apparent. It is tempting to think that the ware being made by the woman in the centre of the image is on a wheel but in fact they

Close-up of the potter.

appear to be two round stones. The scene depicts the making of vessels which have been put to dry before a fire. The finished vessels may be being offered for trade. Rudimentary decoration, the start of ceramic art, is evident.

Pottery making in the Bronze Age and in the Neolithic was more skilled than that seen here; the scene depicts the start of pottery production as Forsyth and Burton imagined it. That is mirrored in the ornament of the border and the symbolism of the image.

THE LIVERPOOL BLITZ AND THE GODDESS OF DESTRUCTION

"The night of 3/4 of May 1941 was, without the slightest doubt, the worst in the city's entire history ... between 23.00 – 03.30 no less than 298 bombers had passed over the target area ... 363 tons of high explosive bombs and 1380 incendiary canisters were dropped ...."[124]

Bryan Perrett records that "several hundred fires raged across the city", water mains collapsed and fire brigades from all over the region and beyond were called in to help. Many public buildings were destroyed "... in William Brown Street the Museum was completely wrecked, part of the Central Library complex was burned out, over 150,000 books being lost in the fire, and the Walker Art Gallery was damaged."[125]

In fact, the museum was not completely destroyed. The exterior façade stood but the inside had been burned to the brick, except, that is, for the tile panels. The authorities had taken the precaution of removing many valuable items before the bombing started but even so, not all items could be removed, in particular, the tile panels.

View of war damage. Courtesy National Museums Liverpool.

The damaged museum lay unattended and closed off from the public for many years though museum staff could find a route through the building. Keith Priestman, Head of Conservation at Liverpool Museum after the war, has provided a moving description of what the scene looked like. Writing of the 1950s after the library had been re-opened, he states:

"To step suddenly from the busy, well-lit interior of the Library, into the desolation of the bombed Museum was like experiencing a time-warp; I was shocked. I descended two or three steps and crossed what had been a foyer, then looking down the length of the Main Hall, which had housed the Egyptian collection, I saw that it was roofless and starkly empty. Above, two rows of Ionic columns still pointed to the sky from which destruction had come, and, at the far end, was the remains of the staircase which had led to the upper floors. On the wall above this was a polychrome tile mural, made by the famous firm of Pilkington's, its rich colours could still be seen where protective timbers had fallen away; all that remained to relieve an otherwise monochrome scene. Perhaps the strangest sight was a pair of black basalt statues of the Egyptian goddess of destruction, Sekhmet. Lion-headed and crowned with the sun's disk, they sat impassively, as they had done thirty centuries earlier, before the temple of Mût at Karnak. Indeed, the whole scene was strangely reminiscent of the ruins of some temple or palace."[126]

The panels were not badly damaged. To a certain extent they had been protected by their location away from the most combustible items in the Museum. Also, the tiles were born of a furnace and so would be much better equipped to withstand heat. However - what then? Why didn't

73

the authorities save the panels?

Liverpool had been one of the chief ports in the country. When the war started, and even before, routine maintenance had been suspended throughout the city. The *Liverpool Museum Bulletin* records:

> "In 1945, therefore, the City Council faced the tremendous task of making good more than six years of arrears of maintenance on all its houses and other buildings."[127]

View of war damage. Courtesy National Museums Liverpool.

Temporary shelters in the city had been built during the war for air raid protection – public shelters for 82,000 people and private shelters for over 705,000. These had to be removed and other properties made good. Labour and materials were in short supply. In addition to this, the social and cultural situation had changed completely. The post-war plans of the Labour government, the desire to build for the welfare of all citizens and above all the need to prioritise work had to be considered.

The *Museum Bulletin* reveals that the city's first priority was the replacement of 3,500 temporary bungalows. A further point is that a licensing system insisted that repairs were to be carried out by the simplest and most readily available materials "even though these did not in every case fully meet the technical requirements of the situation."

The museum was not the only great public institution in Liverpool to have suffered. The library is considered to have suffered the greatest loss of any library in Great Britain during the war, yet in the context of the aftermath of the war it is understandable that these "non-essential" buildings were left until time and resources permitted. It was not until 1954 that a scheme was prepared to reinstate some of the galleries.

The *Museum Bulletin* describes the interior scene as "floorless, roofless, charred shells." In 1955 a report was prepared offering a way forward on the rebuilding. The bulletin records that "such had been the destruction" that the museum could not be reconstructed on its original lines. In fact, the Museums Sub-Committee decided that they would build a new and modern museum. When the original museum had been built it was seen as a storehouse of knowledge. By 1954 it was thought[128] that museums should be places of education and research and should be built to facilitate these aspirations. The open shell of the building presented this opportunity and new building methods and design features could be used.

The damaged stairwell is clearly seen above. Courtesy National Museums Liverpool.

In the course of this rebuilding the walls to which the tile panels were affixed were demolished. An extra floor was put into the space which, even had the tile panels been kept, would have interrupted sight of the panels. This does not mean that significant efforts were not made to save the panels. Keith Priestman tells us that various techniques were considered. The tiles

This is the only known colour photograph taken before the panels were demolished. The date is not known. Courtesy National Museums Liverpool.

View of war damage showing the three floor levels. Courtesy National Museums Liverpool.

could not be prised loose as they were set solid into the walls, exactly as Lawrence Burton described. A scheme to try and free the tiles using acid was considered. It was proposed to drill a series of vertical holes behind the tiles and then use the acid to break down the concrete or fixings. This scheme was abandoned because there was insufficient technical expertise to know what effect the acid would have on the tiles.

Priestman's judgement at the time was that "even had the coloured glazes been unaffected, the porous body of the tiles would have absorbed dissolved salts which could subsequently crystallise and lift the glaze."

A colleague of Keith Priestman at the time, Alan Dodson, MBE, was the Head of Technical Services at the museum. He agrees with Priestman's description and adds that "even to access the panels meant a perilous journey across a plank that had replaced the floor." Dodson also remembers that a cine film was made of the rebuilding of the museum, including the damaged panels, although this has not yet been found.

Lawrence Burton was asked to inspect the tile panels. He was escorted up temporary scaffolding and had to peer under the planking at the tiles. However, even the company that installed them could not propose a means of saving them. He recollects: "I only remember seeing one panel and the tiles were absolutely solid on the backing screed. The only thing that could have been done would have been to cut out the whole wall around the tile panel and, if I remember correctly, this would have cost at least £10,000. This was not a sum that either the company or the museum could contemplate at that time." (The current value of £10,000 is approximately £155,000.)

Priestman recalls that the Museum Principal, Miss Elaine Tankard, made many strenuous efforts to save the work, but to no avail.

The destruction of the panels was a tragedy but one set against the loss of so many lives during the war and the need for so much more vital and essential work.

In 2001 Pilkington's Lancastrian Pottery Society and Salford Museum and Art Gallery were asked to assist in the saving of a 1908 fireplace in a Manchester house. The fireplace is the only surviving installation which has been found featuring Persian tiles designed by John Chambers.

Lawrence Burton hoped that, if the installation had been in 1907/8, then the fireplace would have been "slabbed", i.e., constructed in the factory and then set in place against the wall, and so, removable. This turned out not to be the case. Each tile had been cemented onto the wall and could not be removed individually. In the event, using modern diamond cutting equipment and a full day's work, 56 tiles were saved. The fireplace was subsequently restored and rebuilt as part of the Salford Lifetimes project and has been on public display since 2002. It was perhaps a fifth the size of each of the Liverpool panels and was, of course, easily accessible and not half way up a 30 foot high wall. Even with equivalent technology it would, on a simple arithmetical basis, have taken several months of labour to remove the Liverpool panels in this way. In addition, account must be taken of the necessary recording in minute detail of where every tile had been placed and the care necessary not to damage individual tiles.

The aftermath of the bombing. The tile panels can be seen in the background.
Courtesy National Museums Liverpool.

PILKINGTON'S, A LANCASTRIAN POTTERY

The Pilkington's story[129] is unusual because the company, although named Pilkington's, is really the story of William Burton, his brother Joseph and the artists and craftsmen whom they were able to draw together at the start of the new century.

Certificate of Incorporation

OF THE

Pilkington's Pottery Company,
Limited.

The company's 1891 registration.

Certificate of Incorporation

OF

Pilkington's Tile & Pottery Company,
Limited.

The company's 1892 registration now showing tiles and pottery.

The company monogram, said to have been designed by Lewis F. Day, reflects this energising relationship between the Burtons and the Pilkingtons. In it, the letter "P" reflects the ownership and entrepreneurial vision of the four Pilkington brothers and the two "bees" represent the equal energy and enthusiasm of William and Joseph Burton. They are also the symbol of Manchester.

The generally understood view is that William Burton had been "head-hunted" by the Pilkington brothers who provided venture capital. Burton, then only 28, was a young entrepreneur who could only be recruited once his contract had expired with his previous employers. Indeed, such was the nature of this coup that Pilkington's and Burton were at great pains to keep it secret until the last possible moment.[130] However, Margaret Pilkington, the daughter of one of the original Pilkington founders, states that

"William Burton approached my uncles and my father and interested them in the project and in the financing of the new company."[131]

William Burton's previous employment is described in detail by A.J. Cross.[132] He was an extraordinary figure. He was a "Manchester man" born in Newton Heath and his "network" of contacts is vividly brought to life by Lawrence Burton.[133] He points out that, though now heavily industrialised, at the turn of the century the tile factory was a "green field" site in every sense. It was located in open fields adjacent to the then still clean and pleasant stretch of the River Irwell with nearby canal and railway links.

However, as A.J. Cross explains, it is essential to understand that William Burton was not just an entrepreneur. He had been well educated in science, had attended the Royal School of Mines in Kensington, and had studied "chemistry and the other branches of natural science." Cross tells us that Burton's pottery experience began at Wedgwood's in 1887 where he remained as a chemist for five years. He was also an examiner for the London City and Guilds boards. He lectured extensively and published papers of award-winning acclaim, which culminated in the award of an honorary Master of Arts degree by Manchester University.

Lawrence Burton posed the question: "How did the firm then get started so quickly and so successfully?" He then gave the explanation:

> "A key to understanding this lay with the character of Manchester in the second half of the 19th century. The City's vigour had been epitomised in the energy needed to build the new Manchester Town Hall. Waterhouse's masterpiece had been started by a public subscription to raise £750,000 and by the time the building was completed, over £1,000,000 had been raised to do the

project justice. With this new money, art and the arts in Manchester were stimulated generally. The tiles were by Craven Dunnill (there was a subsequent connection through the Howells who went on to own Craven Dunnill, one of the Howells worked at Pilkington's and was a candidate for William Burton's job when the latter retired) and the murals in the Great Hall were put into the hands of Ford Maddox Brown and Frederick Shields. Shields had a long association with Walter Crane, who came to be the Director of Design at Manchester School of Art in 1893. Both Shields and Crane were to do design work for Pilkington's, with Walter Crane especially having a long connection with the company.

Clifton Junction then, far from being some outpost in the middle of nowhere, was very much a part of this artistic and innovative environment and Manchester energy. As the city expanded, the various building works, of which the town hall was only one, created an enormous demand for tiles. British tileries were recognised as world leaders, so it was not surprising Pilkington's venture should have been into tiles.

In the mid 1890s tile manufacturing was exceedingly viable. Designers like Voysey, Crane, Mucha, and Shields were to work with Pilkington's and many of these worked with other tile companies too. Pilkington's also had a tenuous link with De Morgan, as he bought biscuit pots from Carters of Poole and, many years later, Carters became a subsidiary of Pilkington's."

Lawrence Burton also points out that:

"One factor often forgotten is that Pilkington's was a commercial manufacturer working in profit. Virtually all its pottery competitors were small artistic firms such as De Morgan and Della Robbia, which failed financially; the only competitor comparable to Pilkington's was Doulton, who made pottery as part of its wider ceramic production.

Not only was Pilkington's at this time a successful commercial company, they were also an enlightened one. Forsyth was not just a pottery artist. He designed stained glass, was a leader of artists and also a fine painter. William Burton encouraged a number of the staff to attend night classes at art school and paid for this; two members obtained scholarships to the Royal College of Art, Charles Cundall and Albert Barlow. Both developed into successful artists in their own right. Cundall became a successful R.A. and Barlow, working under the tuition of Johnston, went on to become a successful calligrapher. It was perhaps not surprising that Edward Johnston produced the calligraphy for William Burton's retirement presentation."

This provides a snapshot of the energy running through this new company. Other parts of the tale are told by Cross and Lomax. Pilkington's "lady" artists had also gained reputations enhanced by illustrations of their work in *The Studio*.

Whilst the fame of the company's pottery works was spreading, the company's fame as a tile maker was also growing. Major tile exhibitions at Glasgow, Paris and Wolverhampton had already secured Pilkington's reputation. Pilkington's was fortunate, or Burton was instrumental, in securing other "tile" men.

W.S. Mycock, who later switched from tiles to pottery work, was a capable and respected artist. Edmund Kent, who had worked at Wedgwood, joined the company some three years before the Liverpool work began. Richard Joyce had worked for Moore Brothers and Bretby and it was Bernard Moore who introduced him to Pilkington's. Modellers such as Joseph Kwiatkowski had worked at Wedgwood.

John Chambers, a Doulton and Wedgwood man no doubt drawn by Burton, came as Chief Designer.

Pilkington's had also secured the services of Edward T. Radford whom Bernard Moore described as "one of the best throwers he had ever seen."

Abraham Lomax, who was a dedicated and capable chemist at the factory, working alongside Burton described him as "a man with vision, ability, ideas and abounding energy."[134]

The role of Burton's brother Joseph was also significant. Joseph commenced work at Pilkington's before William could be "released" from Wedgwood's. He was a scientist, Lomax tells us, "particularly in the branches of chemistry, physics and mineralogy." Pilkington's was acknowledged as one of the first of the "scientific" factories able to bring the new discoveries of the age to production. It was Joseph who began the application of scientific production methods to factory work including improvements to kilns and temperature control. He is also recorded as an expert in Chinese Sung and Ming pottery.

By 1913 Pilkington's new discoveries, their perfection of lustre techniques, their extraordinary glaze effects (orange vermilion, kingfisher blue, striated and feathered, opalescent and serpentine) had established their reputation.

Their tile work had become as celebrated as their glazes. In tile design they had secured an early influential champion in Lewis F. Day. Pilkington's range of early printed designs was enormous and its early pattern books feature hundreds of designs. Chambers in particular was noted for his work on tiles in the Persian and Iznik styles. Crane's designs for Pilkington's, such as "Flora's Train", were already celebrated, as were those reproductions of tile panels designed by Alphonse Mucha.

H.C. Marillier, writing for the catalogue of the 1908 Franco-British Exhibition, extolled the way Pilkington's, under the Burtons, had achieved a unity of "artistic value" and "technical skill."

Gordon Mitchell Forsyth, ARCA, RI, FRSA, was born in Aberdeen in 1879. Lomax takes seven pages to describe Forsyth's many attributes. He was not just a gifted artist. He had won scholarships of art in London, travelled extensively, had studied under Gerald Moira and Professor W.R. Lethaby of the Royal College of Art "whose philosophies and approach to teaching would have instilled in Forsyth the 'Arts and Crafts' concerns for craftsmanship and improved design in industry."[135]

Forsyth taught part-time at Manchester Art School from 1912 to 1917. He became a special visitor at the Glasgow School of Art in 1914 and was a regular exhibitor at the Royal Institute of Painters in Watercolour, and at the Royal Academy, in London. Forsyth had had enormous experience before arriving at Pilkington's. He had been Art Director at Minton Hollins and had received calligraphy tutorship under Edward Johnston. Forsyth was a skilled artist in his own right and his work is much sought after. One significant work, which illustrates his abilities in tile design, is his panel of 6 x 6 inch tiles at Manchester Art Gallery. His influence at Pilkington's is significant. He joined the company in 1906 and Lomax informs us that his coaching and encouragement of his staff (he was Head of the Artists) evoked a new "vitality and purpose" in their work. This might be an exaggeration since the artists were all gifted people.

It is more likely, as Cross states that:

> "Under his guidance and leadership the pottery artists at Pilkington's matured into an effective team and Forsyth's contribution to the company's success cannot be overstressed."

Forsyth's enthusiasm for his work is based on his own simple view:

"... you cannot work in clay without learning to love it – always."[136]

In his book *Art and Craft of the Potter* his enthusiasm for teaching is most apparent. Lomax lists the names of the men and women in whom Forsyth "sowed the seeds of art...". These include more than twenty five people who became teachers in schools of art, or designers, at factories such as Minton, Wedgwood, Spode, Shelley and Meakin; or became famous in their own right as potters such as Susie Cooper and Clarice Cliff.

Joseph Burton    Gordon Forsyth    William Burton

Forsyth's monogram

HOW THIS WORK CAME ABOUT

This is a publication of the Pilkington's Lancastrian Pottery Society, which was founded in 1997 with the objectives of promoting "interest in and the study of the history and products of the Pilkington's Factory and its wares".[137]

In the period since 1997 the Society has held five major exhibitions in UK art galleries and has published a quarterly *Newsletter* concerned with Pilkington's tiles and pottery. The Society is greatly strengthened by having as its Chairman Lawrence Burton, a grandson of Joseph Burton, who was also employed at the factory as Sales and Marketing Director from 1951 to 1982. The Society also enjoys the full co-operation of the present factory management. Pilkington's continues today as a modern tile factory, producing, as it did from its beginning, tiles for general, specialised and decorative use.

With the formation of Pilkington's Lancastrian Pottery Society in 1997 interest was again awakened in the cartoons for the Liverpool panels. Within the factory itself the presence of the cartoons, whilst not a secret, was only of interest to a few, including Sylvia Dawes who had worked at the factory since the 1960s, and Lawrence Burton.

It was Sylvia Dawes who first made the existence of the cartoons known to the Society. Lawrence Burton conceived the idea of this publication and, more importantly, of driving forward plans to retrieve the cartoons, have them restored, and placed once again on public view.

The cartoons have not fared well over time. They have been kept rolled up in a very dry and dusty atmosphere. The original intention had been to unroll the cartoons, hang and photograph them but this proved to be impossible. The fact that they had been rolled had preserved the astonishing vibrancy of the colours but the closeness of their rolling had compromised the canvases which had become badly decayed and friable. It proved impossible to hold them vertically and the cramped storage space meant that they had to be photographed horizontally. Some perspective distortion has had to be corrected digitally on several of the illustrations. This is evidenced by a loss of detail in places. In time and after full restoration it is intended to photograph the canvases again.

Lawrence Burton's persistence and the factory's generosity has now resulted in a gift of the cartoons to Salford Museum and Art Gallery where action is in hand to acquire funding towards the full restoration and display of these magnificent paintings.

NOTES

Introduction
1 Furnival, 1904. Burton is quoted extensively.
2 Liverpool Museum and Art Gallery.
http://www.livgrad.co.uk/recorder/Sep97/rec16.html
3 *Liverpool Museum Bulletin,* Vol. 13 (1965-66), p.3.

Liverpool Museum and the Pilkington's connection
4 Ibid., p.4.
5 Ibid., p.9.
6 Ibid., p.16.
7 Ibid., p.16.
8 Minutes of Liverpool City Council, 7th May 1913.
9 A detailed report is contained in the magazine of the Tiles and Architectural Ceramics Society (TACS) *Glazed Expressions* (2003), No. 47, p.16.
10 *The Studio*, subtitled "A Magazine of Fine and Applied Art", first appeared in 1893. It quickly took advantage of the new art of photography and was the "leading international medium of communication between artists". (*Studio International*, incorporating *The Studio*, 75th anniversary edition, Cory, Adams & Mackay, London, 1968, p.170). It also produced an annual yearbook summary.
11 Walter Crane, who is mentioned in the appreciation of the Bluecoat Exhibition, had undertaken early designs for Pilkington's. Some 20 years earlier Crane held enormous influence in the art world and had also been instrumental in establishing the Arts and Crafts Exhibition Society, along with William Morris and others of the Arts and Crafts school. Crane's family came from Liverpool and he had many connections there.
12 *The Studio Yearbook 1908*, p.292.
13 *The Studio,* February 1912, p.52.
14 *The Liverpool Daily Post and Mercury,* 4th June 1913, p.5.
15 *The Manchester Courier,* 14th September 1913.
16 Briggs, Wolstenholme and Thornley were also architects for the White Church, a white faience-tiled church in Lytham St. Annes. The builders of the White Church used tiles provided by the Middleton Brick and Tile Company located a few miles from Pilkington's factory. Perhaps part of that tender process had drawn Pilkington's to their attention. We have not been able to find any public tender advertisements for the work in *The Builder* or *The British Architect* of the time.

The museum's intent
17 Gibson & Wright, 1988.
18 The Mayer gift was catalogued by Gatty in 1883 who divided the antiquities into three styles, namely Byzantine (6th to 12th century), Gothic (13th to 14th century) and Cinquecento (c.1500) ["that style of art which arose in Italy about 1500", *Shorter O.E.D*].
19 Birmingham Museum has very similar features to those of Liverpool. The entrance stairway to the main museum also features a painting at the top of the stairs although in Birmingham's case it is an image from 1914. Birmingham's ceramic gallery is similarly placed around a large floor with a gallery above.
20 *The Architect and Contract Reporter,* Vol. 91 (13th February 1914), p.164.
21 This work is very much a beginning and as yet it has not been possible, due to the current refurbishment, to obtain complete access to all the Liverpool archives. Roger Hall (Research Officer with Liverpool Record Office) has provided the extract from the annual report of the Libraries and Museums Committee. Hall states that the tiles are not mentioned in any further reports between 1915 and 1925.

How the tiles were made and fixed
22 Brett James, a modern potter working in lustre in the Pilkington's style, has highlighted the difficulty of working with these glazes. James informs us that if he were reproducing these panels today he would not use an alkaline glaze because of the difficulties in working with a glaze which is thick and unpredictable.
23. Lomax, 1957, p.46.
24 Forsyth, 1934, p.68.

Choices, costs and delays
25 van Lemmen & Malam, 1991, p 10.
26 Interestingly most of his lists ignore the Americas and the Pacific areas.
27 *The Pottery Gazette,* 1st January 1898, p.104.
28 *The Pottery Gazette,* 1st November 1898, p.1355.
29 *The Pottery Gazette,* 1st November 1900, p.1255.
30 *The Pottery Gazette,* 1st July 1904.

The Babylonian panel
31 Furnival, 1904, p.23.
32 Ibid., p.32.
33 Ibid., p.32.
34 Glazier, 1899; 1995 ed., p.9.
35 Crane, 1902, p.200.
36 Though the design on his lower garment is a series of circles these may be a stylised form of fish-scale pattern. This is another cultural reference to power and magic. Fish scales were common Assyrian images. These represented Enki who was the god of wisdom and water. Enki, or Ea, is represented as a bearded man surrounded by flowing water who, like the king, had magical protective powers.
37 Venetia Porter quotes the classical author Cresias who wrote in the fourth century: "on both the towers and walls are animals of every kind ingeniously executed by the use of colours. The whole had been made to represent a hunt, complete in every detail, of all sorts of wild animals and their size more than four cubits." However she makes the point that these scenes were probably not hunting scenes but "a variety of different animals, some of them mythical." Porter, 1995, p.22.
38 There are examples of these winged bulls in the Louvre. There is a curious unsolved connection with Pilkington's. In the Richard Joyce papers held at Manchester Art Gallery are two water colour sketches signed by Fred Wallenberg annotated "Paris 1896". One is of designs from an Assyrian palace similar to the images in the cartoon. The other is entitled "Genie protecteur tête d'aigle. Palais du roi Asseur Nazir Habal (IX siecle) (Kalakh)." Kal, Kalakh or Calah was an ancient city of Assyria and is the same as the city of Nimrod named after a legendary Assyrian hunting hero. Ashurnasirpal II chose the site as his capital.
39 See www.swan.ac.uk/classics/staff/dg/bsa/bosanquet/bosanquetp.htm. We are grateful to David Gill for this information.
40 Bosanquet was born in 1871 and studied at Cambridge. He was a classical scholar and by 1900 Director of the British School in Athens. In 1906 he became Professor of Classical Archaeology at the University of Liverpool. He resigned from the Museum Sub-Committee in 1915 to work with the Serbian Relief Fund. He remained associated with the University until 1920 and died in 1935. His publication list is extensive and mostly concerned with classical archaeology. No correspondence relating to Pilkington's is known in Professor Bosanquet's papers.
41 Leonard W. King, MA, Litt.D, was an acknowledged scholar and authority on Babylonian and Assyrian history and particularly in the study of cuneiform. He wrote numerous important works, some in collaboration with Sir Wallis Budge who was a keeper of Egyptian and Assyrian antiquities in the British Museum. Interestingly, among the papers sent to us by Patricia Usick, Department of Egyptian Antiquities at the British

Musem, are photocopies of a work by Budge with illustrations similar to Forsyth's figures. Though of a later date (1925) no doubt these illustrations of Ashurnasirpal II, King of Assyria, 883 – 859 BC, were known to Forsyth. Budge states:
"… it is an obvious truth that he [King] published more Sumerian, Babylonian and Assyrian texts than all the other Assyriologists in the world. And the quality of his work was as good as its quantity was great." Budge, 1925, p.178.

The Chinese panel
42 Burton, 1906, pp.46-47.
43 For students of Pilkington's it is especially interesting to read Burton's description of transmutation glazes which were a major feature of Pilkington's 1904 Graves Gallery Exhibition.
44 City of Manchester Art Gallery, *Catalogue of an Exhibition of Chinese Applied Art*. G. Falkner, Manchester, 1913.
45 Fenollosa, 1912; 1963 ed., p.16.
46 For example, in a chapter devoted to feudal art in Japan, Fenollosa discusses the work of the priest Kakuyu better known as Toba Sojo. Fenollosa illustrates a work by Toba Sojo entitled "Battle of the Bulls." The Pilkington's artist W.S. Mycock much later reproduced this work on a vase in sgraffito.
47 Binyon was born in Lancaster and was perhaps more famous as a war poet. Lines from his poem *For the Fallen* are traditionally spoken at Armistice services across Britain.
48 Hobson, 1910.
49 The publishers of that edition have made some observations on the original. In particular they state that so complicated was the original lithographic process it could not be replicated. Some of the colour work required as many as 30 lithographic stones per subject and the average was 19. The colour of the reproduction is very good and in some cases it is quite clear from where Forsyth drew his inspiration. (For students of Pilkington's ware the book might almost be seen as a source book as so many of the shapes and themes are recognisable in Pilkington's shapes and glazes.)
50 Bushell,1897-99; 1981 ed., p.67.
51 Ibid., p.62.
52 Ibid., p.68.
53 Ibid., p.67.
54 Ibid., p.298.
55 Laing & Wire, 1993, p.144.
56 Bushell, 1897-99, 1981 ed., p.11.
57 City of Manchester Art Gallery, *Catalogue of an Exhibition of Chinese Applied Art*. G. Falkner, Manchester, 1913.

The Persian panel
58 Pemberton, H.M., "Some Modern Pottery", *The Art Journal*, 1911, p.119.
59 Caiger-Smith, 1985, provides an excellent "modern" account.
60 Wallis, 1894, p.2.
61 Furnival, 1904, p.84, quotes an extract from *The Sentinel*, 23rd February 1891.
62 *The Pottery Gazette*, 1st January 1923, p.95.
63 Lomax, 1957.
64 Ibid., p.78.
65 Cross, 1980, p.21.
66 The work of John Chambers needs further study. Many examples of his work and of Pilkington's lustre pottery are now on public view thanks to the generosity of his late children Mary and Arthur.
67 A Lancaster University information leaflet cites Owen Jones' *Grammar of Ornament* as a source work for these designs.
68 Riley, 1987, p.19.

69 Caiger-Smith, 1985, p.80.

70 Richard Gray, who is now Director at Compton Verney Museum in South Warwickshire, informs us that the photograph came from archives held at the factory in 1979. Forsyth is seen wearing a hat. The other artists are not identified though the worker closest to the canvas bears a resemblance to David Evans, an artist at Pilkington's. The other workers are exceedingly young and one appears to be a small boy. The picture is a scan of that exhibition image.

71 Grey, B. *Persian Painting*, illustrated p.103. *The Bulletin of the Cleveland Museum of Art*, (December 1956, p.214) records that the page was part of a frontispiece to a copy of a Persian epic poem written by the poet Firdawsi at the end of the tenth century. It was acquired from the Chester Beatty collection which was established in Dublin in 1956, although Beatty had lived in London in 1910. The museum accession notes state "scenes like this ...are frequently used as frontispieces in Persian manuscripts." (Object sheet 1945.169). The same bulletin states that the scholar W.P. Schulz also brought a copy of this work to Germany in 1899 and that the Bibliothèque Nationale Paris holds a further copy acquired in 1833. The work was well known to scholars. Reference is also made to the John Rylands Library in Manchester and its collection of Persian manuscripts. The Rylands has a collection of about 950 items on paper, chiefly originating from the Crawford purchase of 1901. By 1910 it was well established as an institution of international renown. A later work by B.W. Robinson ("Some Illustrated Persian Manuscripts in the John Rylands Library" notes the similar images in the style of the frontispiece amongst the miniatures in the Rylands collection. Taken from:
Catalogue entry:Author:Robinson, B. W. (Basil William) Title:Some illustrated Persian manuscripts in the John Rylands Library. In:John Rylands Library. Abbreviated title Bull. John Rylands Libr. Bulletin of the John Rylands Library. -- Manchester, Manchester University Press [etc.] 1951. 27 cm. v. 34 (1951) p. 69-80. plates. ISSN 0021-7239.
Research into the connection with Forsyth or Burton continues.

72 Walter Crane lived for a while near Holland Park in London and designed part of the frieze for the Arab Hall in Lord Leighton's House - around the corner. (The capitals were designed by Randolph Caldecott, another Manchester artist.) William De Morgan designed some of the replacement tiles and much of the "new" tilework to accompany the Persian antiquities. It is more than likely that several of the Pilkington's artists were familiar with the house and its tile panels, which inevitably are reminiscent of some of the Persian motifs.

73 Crane, 1902, p.210.

74 http://islamicceramics.ashmol.ox.ac.uk/Iznik/timeline.htm

75 Yamanlar-Mizuno, Toa University:
http://www.l.u-tokyo.ac.jp/IAS/HP-e2/eventreports/32saray7.html

76 Lillys et al., 1965, pp.96 & 110.

77 Crane, 1902, p.40.

78 Burton, 1906, p.68.

79 Ibid., p.68.

80 Fehervari, 1973, p.144.

81 Ibid., p.149.

82. The Manchester catalogue describes art work by Richard Joyce in a similar style. Though this work is later it would seem that the artists perhaps all worked on the Persian panel. A panel by Forsyth is currently on exhibition at Manchester Art Gallery and another Joyce tile is illustrated here. A less well known figure at Pilkington's, Albert Barlow, designed an illuminated roundel and a tile panel. Barlow went on to become a skilled calligrapher and enjoyed success in this field. Mycock kept numerous items taken from magazines and newspapers which served as inspiration for his work. Amongst these are several pages from *The Connoisseur* magazine entitled "Notable Collections – A Rhodian Ware Collection" by Leonard Willoughby and dated 1911. There are illustrations and several plates that might have inspired the artists. Salford Museum and Art Gallery have an ephemera archive related to W.S. Mycock.

The Greek panel
83 "Pupils need Greek myths ...," Lord Quirk, Adviser to the Specialist Schools Trust, *The Independent*, 30th June 2003.
84 Crane, 1902, p.204.
85 Furnival, 1904, p.50.
86 Lane, 1971, p.16.
87 Cross, 1980, p.49. This drinking cup is illustrated by Cross who compares it with a similar image on a Pilkington's kylix dated 1906.

The Roman panel
88 Letter dated 2nd December 1914.
89 Grimes, W.F. "Holt, Denbighshire, the works-depôt of the Twentieth Legion at Castle Lyons". *Y Cymmrodor*, Vol.41(1930),p.34.
Holt was a vary large site and unusual in its size. Swan (*The Pottery Kilns of Roman Britain* HMSO, London, 1984, p.95) says: "this was perhaps because they used saggars - this was unique to Holt where they were connected with the production of lead-glazed wares - which took up a great deal of space." Also unique to Holt was a woodstore which was possibly covered. Holt also had the most elaborate drying plant known in Roman Britain.
Dan Robinson of the Grosvenor Museum, Chester, has provided the following information: "The definitive publication on the Holt pottery appeared in Volume XLI of *Y Cymmrodor*, the magazine of the Honourable Society of Cymmrodorion. The paper, which fills the whole volume, is called "Holt, Denbighshire; the works depot of the Twentieth Legion at Castle Lyons" by W.F. Grimes, MA; it was published in 1930. Grimes made his name from this work, which was basically to put together the research of T.A. Acton - Arthur Acton - in an accessible form. Acton died in 1925 before he could complete his work. The vast majority of the finds went to the National Museum of Wales in Cardiff, although we have a few typical pieces loaned to us by them."
90 Grimes, 1930, pp.24 & 31.
91 Mayer, 1871, p.32.
92 *The Pottery Gazette*, 1st November 1900.
93 Boardman, J., *The Kilns of Ancient Rome* in Camusso and Bortone, 1991, pp.89-97.
94 Johns, 1971.
95 Furnival, 1904, p.66.

The panels that never happened
96 In an interview in *The Pottery Gazette*, 1st February 1906, p.188.
97 De Morgan, W., "Lustre Ware", *Journal of the Society of Arts*, Vol. 40 (1892). He delivered the paper to the Society on 31st May 1892. It is available at:
www.tiles.org/pages/wdm/wdmlustr.htm
98 *The Pottery Gazette*, 1st January 1923, p.95.
99 p.153 of Fourest, H.P., *European Majolica* in Camusso & Bortone, 1991, pp.150-217.
100 Pilkington's did not produce much ware with a bas-relief. The most famous example is a large modelled plaque of Saint George slaying the dragon. (See illustration in Lomax.)
101 Furnival, 1904, p. 152.
102 *The American Pottery Gazette*, June 1907, p.28.
103 Ms. Anabella Wake, Adelaide, South Australia (Society for Creative Anachronism: Lady Bella Lucia da Verona, Barony of Innilgard, Lochac)
Website: The Realm of Venus: http://realmofvenus.renaissancewoman.net
104 This is in a letter dated 26th January 1914 from Mr. Entwistle to Mr. Burton.
105 Forsyth, 1904, p.51.
106 Godden, 1974, p.110.
107 Frit is a ground glass or glaze which ensures uniformity of colour and the final glaze effect.
108 Burton, 1904.

109 Burton, 1922. In the acknowledgement to this work Burton thanks Bernard Rackham of the Victoria and Albert Museum for "much" assistance in the selection of specimens for his work. The V & A have a significant amount of Liverpool ware. One bowl in the collection was used to illustrate a cigarette card series devoted to "old potters".
110 *National Museums Liverpool Maritime Archives & Library Information Sheet No.27,* revised 2003.
111 Barnard, 1972.
112 Ibid., p.12.
113 The TACS website lists over 50 important tile installations in Liverpool buildings but only one specific reference to Pilkington's. This is for the Lister Drive Baths which must have been a favourite commission of Burton because he specifically mentions this work in conversation with a *Pottery Gazette* reporter in 1900.
114 Riley, 1987, p.74.
115 Brown, 1996.
116 *Glazed Expressions* , No. 45 (2002).
117 F.J. Leslie quoted in "Everton in the old days", *Esmeduna,* April 1911. (http://www.parry3654.freeserve.co.uk/Everton.htm)
118 *The Pottery Gazette,* 1st November 1897.
119 Day, 1903, p.2.
120 Ibid., p.3.
121 The archaeologist Howard Austin has suggested that the people represented might be "beaker people". Austin writes: "*About 2500 BC an influx of migrants settled in Britain. These newcomers have been called the 'Beaker People' because of the shape of the pottery vessels which are so often found in their round barrow graves. The newcomers who appear to be of a much stockier build, although few at first, seem to have quickly gotten the upper hand on their Neolithic landlords, becoming a sort of nouveau aristocracy.*
The Beaker Folk were farmers and archers, wearing stone wrist guards to protect their arms from the sting of the bowstring. They were also the first metal smiths in England, working first in copper and gold, and later in the bronze which has given its name to this era".
122 It has been confirmed that the images and head-dresses in this panel are not those of the Pueblo.
123 Forsyth, 1934, p.34.

The Liverpool blitz and the Goddess of Destruction
124 Perrett, 1990.
125 Ibid., p.98.
126 From a book in progress *Those Museum Days,* an account of the museum in the 1950s and 60s, by Keith Priestman, formerly Head of Conservation, Liverpool Museum.
127 *Liverpool Museum Bulletin,* Vol. 13 (1965-66), p.17.
128 Author: Liverpool. Public Libraries, Museums and Art Gallery. Title: *The destruction of the Liverpool City Museums A review of events*, by Douglas A. Allan. In: Museums Journal, Vol. 41, pp. 55 and 105-107, pl. 5, 1941.

Pilkington's, a Lancastrian pottery
129 Pilkington's Pottery Company was formally incorporated on 24th January 1891. The company was originally established to produce tiles which may account for the registered change of name to "Pilkington's Tile & Pottery Company" on 18th January 1892. This is only a summary. There are two significant works which give much more detail. In 1957 Abraham Lomax published his own personal account of his time at the factory as chemist between 1896 and 1911. In 1980 A.J. Cross published a thorough and detailed study of the pottery and its achievements, illustrated profusely with examples of Pilkington's pottery and tile ware. Cross' book is available today and is the recognised "modern" work concerned with the factory. Pilkington's Lancastrian Pottery Society has produced a bibliographic list of references to Pilkington's which details over 200 references.

130 Unpublished letter, Pilkington's archives, May 1892.
131 Unpublished letter from Margaret Pilkington to Frank Mullineux (Curator, Monks Hall Museum, Eccles), 1968.
132 Cross, 1980.
133 *Pilkington's Lancastrian Pottery Society Newsletter* (1997), No.1.
134 Lomax, 1957, p.88.
135 Aberdeen Art Gallery, *Artist as Educator: Gordon Mitchell Forsyth (1872 – 1952)*. Aberdeen Art Gallery, Aberdeen, 1994.
136 Forsyth, 1934, p.97.
137 Constitution of Pilkington's Lancastrian Pottery Society, 1997.

ACKNOWLEDGEMENTS

The Society is most grateful for the help and assistance given by the following organisations and individuals:

Pilkington's Tiles Ltd. without whom this publication would have been impossible. They allowed us to photograph the cartoons whilst they were still at the factory and to make notes from archival records. After serious consideration as to the future of the cartoons, the factory very generously donated them to Salford Museum and Art Gallery so that they can be conserved and ultimately put on public display.

Salford Museum and Art Gallery who have supported this publication and who are arranging for the restoration of the cartoons.

National Museums Liverpool who have provided information and given us permission to reproduce images from their collection. Special thanks are due to Sue Lunt, Senior Curator, and Pauline Rushton. Also Keith Priestman formerly Head of Conservation at the museum, who has helped considerably with eye-witness accounts.

Lancaster University Rare Book Archive and the Peter Scott Gallery who have very generously provided their time and allowed us access to the recently donated Chambers papers.

Individuals at several museums have also been very helpful. We are most grateful to Patricia Usick of the British Museum for information concerning Leonard King and to Dan Robinson of the Grosvenor Museum in Chester for information concerning the Holt excavations.

Lawrence Burton, a direct descendent of Joseph Burton and Sales and Marketing Director at Pilkington's from 1951 to 1982.

Our thanks also to John Henson, Richard Burns, Judy & Bob Sandling and A.J. Cross whose own book *Pilkington's Royal Lancastrian Pottery and Tiles* has provided much information and inspiration. Judy in particular has been a patient and informed critic.

The Society also acknowledges the interest and help given by the Tiles and Architectural Ceramics Society (TACS) to this venture. TACS helped with the initial outline of research and has shared our enthusiasm to record these unique pieces of ceramic art.

Martin Diggle of Teknigrafiks has corrected or re-imaged the photographs of the cartoons to compensate for the poor and partly torn originals and for the distortion of perspective. That the images are so vibrant is a tribute to his hours of effort on our behalf.

Our most grateful thanks must go to the committee and members of the Pilkington's Lancastrian Pottery Society.

Finally our thanks are due especially to Ian Pringle, Dip.A.D., who very generously spent hours of his time reviewing our text and offering particular insights.

PHOTOGRAPHIC ACKNOWLEDGEMENTS

All cartoon images are copyright Pilkington's Tiles Ltd. and as below.
Pages 1, 6, 7, 8, 24, 25, 27, 29, 30, 32, 33 upper, 48 lower, 51, 53, 55, 57, 60, 61, 63, 70, 71, 72, 81, 94. Copyright A. & B. Corbett.
Pages 10, 14, 17, 23, 26 upper, 28, 33 lower, 36, 37, 38, 49, 54, 66, 67, 73, 74, 75, 76, 77. Copyright & courtesy National Museums Liverpool.
Pages 24, 32, 51, 57, 61, 71. Digitally enhanced images copyright Teknigrafiks.
Page 39. Copyright & courtesy Cleveland Museum of Art, Ohio.
Pages 26 lower, 42. Copyright & courtesy Manchester Art Gallery.
Page 24, 32, 43, 51, 57, 61, 63, 71. Copyright & courtesy Salford Museum & Art Gallery.
Pages 31, 46 lower right, 50, 56. Courtesy of the Rare Book Archive, Lancaster University.
Page 46 upper two & lower left private collection.

SELECT BIBLIOGRAPHY

Ashton, L. & Gray, B. *Chinese Art.* Faber & Faber, London, 1935
Austwick, J. & B. *The Decorated Tile.* Pitman House, London, 1980
Barnard, J. *Victorian Ceramic Tiles.* Studio Vista, London, 1972
Binyon, L. *Painting in the Far East.* E.Arnold, London, 1908; fourth edition reprinted Dover, New York, 1969
Brown, E.M. *The Art of the Potter.* National Museums and Galleries on Merseyside, Liverpool, 1996
Budge, E.A.W. *The Rise and Progress of Assyriology.* Martin Hopkinson, London, 1925
Burton, W. *English Earthenware and Stoneware.* Cassell, London, 1904
Burton, W. *Porcelain, A Sketch of its Nature Art and Manufacture.* Cassell, London, 1906
Burton, W. *Josiah Wedgwood and his Pottery.* Cassell, London, 1922
Bushell, S.W. *Oriental Ceramic Art.* Appleton, New York, 1897-1899 in 10 volumes in a limited edition of 500 ; reprinted: Muller, London, 1981
Caiger-Smith, A. *Lustre Pottery.* Herbert Press, London, 1985
Camusso, L. & Bortone, S. *Ceramics of the World.* Macdonald Illustrated, London, 1991
Crane, W. *The Bases of Design.* G. Bell & Sons, London, 1902
Crane, W. *An Artist's Reminiscences.* Macmillan, New York, 1907
Cross, A.J. *Pilkington's Royal Lancastrian Pottery and Tiles.* Richard Dennis, London, 1980
Day, L.F. *Pattern Design.* Batsford, London, 1903
Day, L.F. *Ornament and its Application.* Batsford, London, 1904
Fehervari, G. *Ceramics of the Islamic World.* Faber and Faber, London, 1973
Fenollosa, E.F. *Epochs of Chinese and Japanese Art. Vol.1.* Heinemann, London, 1899; second edition reprinted: Dover, New York, 1963
Forsyth, G.M. *Art and Craft of the Potter.* Chapman & Hall, London, 1934
Furnival, W.J. *Leadless Decorative Tiles, Faience, and Mosaic.* [Author], Stowe, Staffs., 1904
Gibson, M. & Wright, S. (eds.) *Joseph Mayer of Liverpool 1803 – 1886.* Society of Antiquaries of London & National Museums & Galleries on Merseyside, London, 1988
Glazier, R. *A Manual of Historic Ornament.* Batsford, London, 1899; reprinted as: *The Wordsworth Manual of Ornament.* Wordsworth, Ware, 1995
Godden, G.A. *British Pottery.* Barrie & Jenkins, London, 1974
Grey, Basil. *Persian Painting.* MacMillan, London, 1977
Hobson, R.L. *Exhibition of Early Chinese Pottery and Porcelain.* Burlington Fine Arts Club, London, 1910
Johns, C. *Arretine and Samian Pottery.* British Museum, London, 1971
Jones, O. *The Grammar of Ornament.* Day & Son, London, 1856; reprinted: Studio Editions, London, 1986

Jones, O. *Examples of Chinese ornament selected from objects in the South Kensington Museum and other collections. 1867.*; reprinted as *The Grammar of Chinese Ornament.* Studio Editions, London, 1987
Laing, J. & Wire, D. *The Encyclopaedia of Signs and Symbols.* Studio Editions, London, 1993
Lane, A. *Greek Pottery.* Third edition. Faber and Faber, London, 1971
Laufer, B. *Chinese Pottery of the Han Dynasty.* E.J. Brill, Leiden, 1909; reprinted: C.Tuttle, Rutland, Vermont & Tokyo, Japan, 1962
Leslie, F.J. "Everton in the old days," *Esmeduna,* April 1911 (http://www.parry3654.freeeserve.co.uk/Everton.htm)
Lévèque, J.J. & Ménant, N. *Islamic and Indian Painting.* Heron, London, 1970
Lillys, W., Reiff, R. & Esin, E. *Oriental Miniatures: Persian, Indian, Turkish.* Tuttle, London, 1965
Lockett, T.A. *Collecting Victorian Tiles.* Antique Collectors Club, Woodbridge, 1979
Lomax, A. *Royal Lancastrian Pottery, 1900 –1938.* [Author], Bolton, 1957
Mayer, J. *History of the Art of Pottery in Liverpool.* Maples, Liverpool, 1871
Perrett, B. *Liverpool – A City at War.* Robert Hale, London, 1990
Porter, V. *Islamic Tiles.* British Museum Press, London, 1995
Rhead, G.W. *Modern Practical Design.* Batsford, London, 1912
Riley, N. *Tile Art.* Apple, Baldock, 1987
Smith, G. & Hyde, S. (eds.) *Walter Crane 1845 – 1915.* Lund Humphries & The Whitworth Art Gallery, University of Manchester, London, 1989
van Lemmen, H. & Malam, J. (eds.) *Fired Earth: 1000 Years of Tiles in Europe.* TACS & Richard Dennis, London 1991
Wallis, H. *The Godman Collection. Persian Ceramic Art Belonging to Mr. F. Du Cane Godman. The Thirteenth Century Lustred Wall-Tiles.* [Author], London, 1894

Museum and Exhibition Catalogues

Aberdeen Art Gallery *Artist as Educator: Gordon Mitchell Forsyth (1872 – 1952).* Aberdeen Art Gallery, Aberdeen, 1994
City of Manchester Art Gallery *Catalogue of an Exhibition of Chinese Applied Art.* G. Falkner, Manchester, 1913
Gatty, C.T. *Catalogue of Medieval and Later Antiquities Contained in the Mayer Museum.* G. Walmsley, Liverpool, 1883
Dumas, F.G. (ed.) *The Franco-British Exhibition: Illustrated Review, 1908.* Chatto & Windus, London, 1908

Internet references of interest

Liverpool and Bosanquet:
www.swan.ac.uk/classics/staff/dg/bsa/bosanquet/bosanquetp.htm
Liverpool history: http://www.parry3654.freeeserve.co.uk/Everton.htm
Lustre ceramics: http://islamicceramics.ashmol.ox.ac.uk/Iznik/timeline.htm
Italian Renaissance: http://realmofvenus.renaissancewoman.net
Persian ceramics: http://www.l.u-tokyo.ac.jp/IAS/HP-e2/eventreports/32saray7.html
Yamanlar-Mizuno, Toa University:
http://www.l.u-tokyo.ac.jp/IAS/HP-e2/eventreports/32saray7.html
Islamic pottery. Ashmolean Museum:
http://ashweb.ashmol.ox.ac.uk/ash/departments/eastern-art
Persian miniatures, Cleveland Museum of Art: http://www.clevelandart.org/Explore/
Peter Scott Gallery: www.lancs.ac.uk/users/peterscott/index.htm
and especially
Pilkington's Lancastrian Pottery Society:
http://www.pilkpotsoc.freeserve.co.uk/index.htm

PLANS OF THE MUSEUM

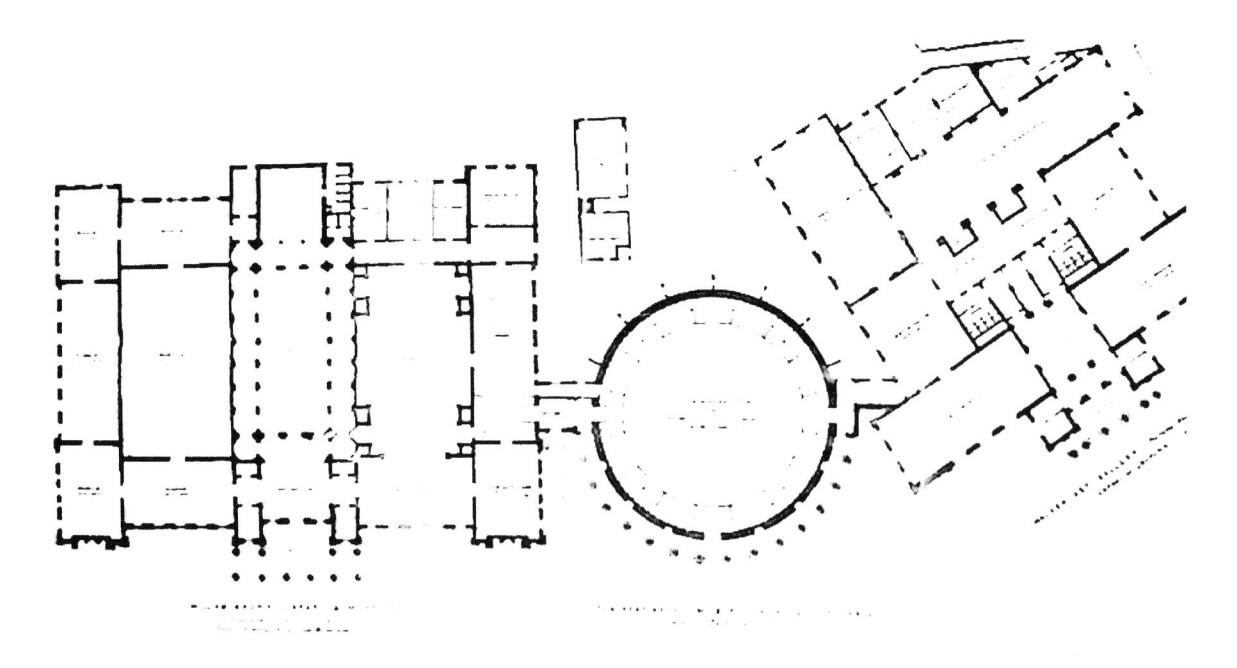

The above plan shows the museum in relation to the library, the circular Picton reading room and the Walker Art Gallery (both Cornelius Sherlock Arch^t.). The museum is to the extreme left of the plan and the Egyptian Gallery was located behind the entrance portico to the museum. The panels were located on the stairwell at the back of the building - detailed below.

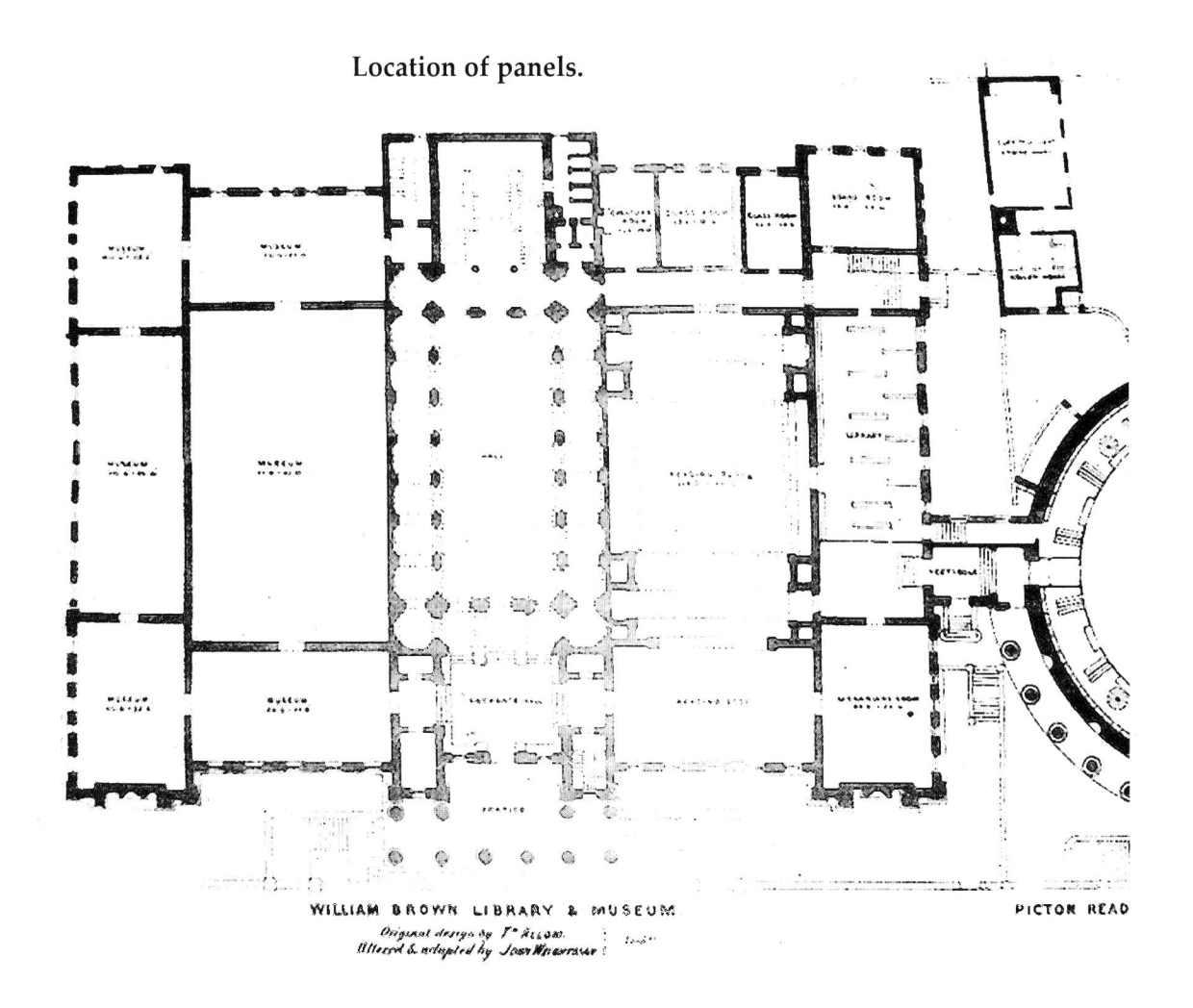

Location of panels.